Future Builders 3166

CHILDREN AT PLAY

Children at Play

DAVID PORTER

KINGSWAY PUBLICATIONS
EASTBOURNE

Biblical quotations are from the
New International Version © International Bible
Society 1973, 1978, 1984.

Front cover photo: Zefa Picture Library

British Library Cataloguing in Publication Data

Porter, David, 1945–
    Children at play.
    1. Children. Development.
        Role of use of toys
    I. Title
    155.4'18

ISBN 0-86065-787-6

Printed in Great Britain for
KINGSWAY PUBLICATIONS LTD
1 St Anne's Road, Eastbourne, E Sussex BN21 3UN by
Richard Clay Ltd, Bungay, Suffolk.
Typeset by Nuprint Ltd, Harpenden, Herts AL5 4SE.

This book is dedicated to
my mother, and to the memory of my father,
with love and admiration.

Contents

Introduction

The voice on the phone sounded sensible and concerned. 'We have just come back to England after four years away, and we're horrified. The toyshops and newsagents seem to be full of really awful things. Has it all happened while we were away, or didn't we notice it before? We aren't at all sure how to handle it. Do we forbid our children to visit toyshops, or what?'

She was telephoning in response to a magazine article I'd written about toys. It was clear from what she said that she wasn't the kind of parent who wanted to wrap her children in cotton wool. She knew her children would have to make their own choices as they grew older, and she was deeply concerned to know how best to help them learn to do so.

Much the same could be said of a couple I know who have a young family. They handed me *Haunted Wood*,[1] an attractively packaged game from a quite reputable manufacturer of quality children's toys. 'For your files,' they said. 'We bought it for a Christmas present. But when we got it home and looked at it, it was just too scary. What *does* one do?'

I accepted the beautifully-presented game, 'full of ghosts and goblins', and I could see the problem.

It wasn't a clear-cut matter. Certainly the game (which was an elaborate variant of Ludo, with cartoon ghosts and monsters illustrating the board) would have been too much for many children I know in the 5–10 year age range suggested by the box. On the other hand, the manufacturers (the highly respected Ravensburger) would certainly have pointed out that the game involves the idea of co-operation in adversity—your pieces have to help each other past obstacles—and that the cartoon nasties are deliberately drawn in a style similar to TV's *Will o' the Wisp*—humorous and, for many children, intriguing and enjoyably spooky rather than frightening and occult-flavoured.

But where does one draw the line? And what is the difference between a child's legitimate fascination with the bizarre, shivery and spine-tingling—and the kind of near-obsession tapped by many sectors of the toy industry, where these interests are the opening that many manufacturers are seeking, who see children as an immensely profitable market ripe for exploitation?

Horror and fantasy are only two of many areas of children's play today where there is much concern. I have encountered that concern as I have spoken to parents, teachers, church organisations, youth groups, conferences, and radio phone-ins—often as a result of interest in my earlier book, *Children at Risk*.[2] In that book I discussed a number of areas in which children today are exposed to risks which are often not obvious. Invitations to speak, letters from total strangers, and many telephone calls confirmed that a significant number of parents and teachers shared my own concerns.

Children at Play, however, is a different book from *Children at Risk*, which is still in print in a second, revised edition.

Children at Play is neither a replacement nor an update. It is not primarily about risks but about influences. Its main emphasis is not *how* children are influenced but *what* influences them. To explore the fascinating subject of child psychology and child development you will need to look elsewhere. (The Notes at the end of this book include some useful titles as a starting point.)

We'll be looking at several areas of toys, games and recreation that contribute to the way a growing child learns to look at the world. It may seem odd to think that a doll or a cuddly toy could be a vehicle for attitudes, values and even ideas, but we will see in the chapters which follow that they are.

Just as with *Children at Risk*, I write as somebody who is both fond of children and interested in the things they play with. As a parent, I want my children's imaginations to be enriched by the wonderful varied strangeness not only of fantasy books but also of many games and toys. I don't think, either, that there are many quick and easy answers to the questions that are often raised.

For example, many parents have told me that they are worried because their children, usually their sons, enjoy playing with guns and toys of violence. It's a much-discussed topic, and arguments for and against have been put forward. They cannot be neatly and quickly resolved. There is no cure-all solution that can be applied to deal with the problem once and for all.

Attempts to find ways of directing children's play so that conflict in any shape or form is avoided are not necessarily in the best interests of the child. Indeed, I believe that whatever view one adopts about violent toys, resolving conflict is one of the most important lessons that group play teaches a child. That is one of the areas we will be considering later.

I have written this book because I share many of the questions that parents and teachers have expressed about modern play. As parents of two children, one just five and the other eleven, I and my wife are faced daily with choices which are often difficult.

For example: do we allow our older daughter to spend her money on something we think might influence her in a harmful way—perhaps a magazine or a music cassette by an artiste we dislike? And do we allow our five-year-old to spend hers on a junk toy which is blatantly cheap and exploitative, but which has captivated her heart and soul?

If we say no to the older daughter, at what stage do we begin to help her make her own choices about what she buys—which she will have to do in a few short years anyway, when she leaves home and begins her adult life? And if we say no to the younger because we really feel there are problems in a particular toy, what do we do about the fact that most of the children in her class at school will probably have the toy she wants, and will let her play with it?

Parenting, teaching, or being involved with a growing child in any way at all is a great privilege. But for many today, faced with toyshops, newsagents and high street stores full of what seem to be quite unsuitable products, it can also seem a sometimes unbearable responsibility.

So I approach this subject aware that in many areas of a child's world, about which I am otherwise very positive, there are problems. Consequently, I want to find an acceptable middle course between the joys and the perils. And I believe that it is possible to do this.

I am writing as a Christian, but I believe that this is a task shared not just by Christians but by all who care about children. On these issues, most people's agendas coincide. We want the very best for our children; we are angry when they are exploited and we want to steer them away from anything that represents a threat to their safety and to their growing up into personal fulfilment and self-acceptance.

I encountered this shared concern when *Children at Risk* was published in 1986. For example, some computer magazines, reviewing the book, pointed out a number of other areas where they themselves saw problems. A long and thoughtful correspondence with a senior member of one of the country's leading fantasy game publishers made me realise that many people in that industry care deeply about children.

Some of the concerns are very recent. In the past two or

three years a number of television documentaries have explored such issues as violent toys, sexist toys, and toys which have been accused of making children grow up too fast (for example, toy cosmetics for young girls). Other similar issues have been widely discussed in the media, and some new and related problems, which simply did not exist a few years ago, have also provoked often heated argument.

One example is telephone chat-lines, where several people can dial a central number independently and find themselves in a group conversation—a variant of the 'conferencing' facility available to business users. Many parents have found chat-lines an extremely expensive (and often unsuspected) hobby for their children, when the bills came in.

Another example is telephone dial-up services, which offer to all and sundry (including children who happen to pick up their parents' newspapers unobserved) the opportunity to dial a number and listen to sexual fantasies or 'advice' on a range of sexual matters. At 25 pence per minute, this is also an expensive pastime.

In 1988 the Government took action against chat-lines, but left the dial-up services alone. In March 1989 the worst of the dial-up services, which were offering pornography, came under restraint. But a wide range of material which is clearly unsuitable for children remained particularly accessible to them, as there is no way of determining the age of the caller. There has been widespread concern about this risk, and in Chapter 9 it is discussed in more detail.

The debate is well under way in the Christian community, too. There is a new interest in the risks that children's play may present. Books have been published which argue that sinister occult and New Age motives lie behind the design of some of the best-loved toys and dolls. A whole lobby within Christian education has rejected any kind of fantasy in a child's curriculum, whether it be *Star Wars* models, Superman comics or the Narnia tales of C.S. Lewis. Other Christian educationalists take a diametrically opposite view. And there are many points of view in between.

Children at Play is intended to be of use in three ways. Firstly, it is *a handbook of information*. It contains information and facts and figures which I hope will be useful as a source of reference. My information is taken from my researches in published material, and many conversations with professionals and others involved with caring for children. I have also been able to talk with people working in the toy and game industry, and their insights are included where appropriate.

Secondly, it is *a guidebook for concerned parents*. If there are bad influences in today's world of children's play, how can we best help our children? What can we do, as parents or teachers or as people otherwise involved with children, to remove dangers out of their way or equip them to deal with what they cannot avoid?

Thirdly, it is *a manifesto for action*. Often it is possible to take constructive steps to request those responsible for manufacturing, distributing, or otherwise promoting the things that cause us concern. We'll be looking at how to go about it, what organisations and statutory authorities exist to help us, and how best to achieve results. The last chapter in particular provides useful names and addresses.

Readers of *Children at Risk* will recognise these three aims as being the same as in the earlier book. *Children at Play* shares the same overall purpose: not to urge an austere bleakness, a depriving of fun and play and a starving of the child's various emotional and even spiritual needs; but to urge an informed caring, a protecting of our children that at the same time prepares them to live in this confused and wonderful world, and which above all preserves their childhood years in a world in which it is all too easy to rob children of childhood.

I would like to add a word about my use of sources. I have tried to ensure that nobody is quoted out of context (with the exception of the quote at the head of Chapter 3, for which I hope Aldous Huxley's admirers will forgive me), and I have documented my sources in the notes, which are fairly detailed. My reason is that I hope that readers will want to read further in some of the material I have been working with.

When I quote from writers on child development and child psychology, I do so without intending to analyse those writers in depth. In preparing this book I have read a number of texts in the field and talked with a number of professionals. But my training is not in child psychology or child development, and when I quote—for example—Bruno Bettelheim, I am not implying that Bettelheim's view of children is necessarily the same as my own. I am simply affirming that the passage I have quoted is an insight into childhood which I have found helpful, from a writer whose opinions I greatly respect. It is not intended that my sources, taken together, should be assumed to add up to a comprehensive view of childhood. They are simply writers whose work I have found helpful, and I share them with you.

The list of people who have helped me in my research is a long one. In particular, this book owes much to Ros Draper who is involved in a number of areas of family therapy, Andy Butcher who was until 1989 editor of *Christian Family*, Sue Byrde, Boopie Cope, Peter Elsom, Edward England, Ursula Harris, Mark Harvey, Richard and Jane Winter, Martyn Eden and the staff of the London Institute for Contemporary Christianity, various members of the staff of CARE Trust and the Evangelical Alliance, and the staff of Greatham School. I have also had valuable help from my local library in Petersfield and the City Business Library in the City of London. A major contribution has been made by all the people who have written to me or telephoned, and those who have taken part in discussion at various meetings.

The greatest contribution of all has been that of my wife Tricia, my partner in the task of parenting.

Any faults in this book are not, however, the responsibility of those mentioned above, and the views expressed and positions adopted should not be assumed to be those of the people and organisations who have helped me.

DAVID PORTER
Greatham, 1989

A Note on Language

Like every other writer on children, I have had to tackle the problem of whether to use 'him' or 'her', or to use an alternative method, when referring to the child in general.

I heartily agree with those people who resent the thoughtless use of 'he' whenever male *and* female are meant. I often wonder how I would feel about such language if I were a female instead of a male. I can see no good reason for dropping 'mankind' as a term for humanity as a whole, but I cannot see any reason either why, when individuals are meant, an author should choose to ignore over half the human race.

Unfortunately, the alternatives I have used in this book are all less than satisfactory. I have chosen to refer to babies as 'it', but as a parent myself I can remember that I would not have been thrilled if anybody had called a baby of mine an 'it'. For older children, I was attracted by Dorothy Einon's device of using 'he' and 'she' in alternate chapters;[1] but the subject coverage of the present book would probably lead to some inappropriate usages, especially where topics such as sexism in toys are under discussion. And whatever else, I was determined to use 'he or she' and other such ugly concoctions very sparingly.

In the end, I have opted for a mixture of genders in my examples, rather than a strict alternation between chapters, and used the plural 'children' where possible. It may be that

I have inadvertently overemphasised boys, or in some way short-changed girls. If so, I apologise in advance. It is a difficult problem, but one that every writer ought to continue to grapple with. Blame it not on prejudice or laziness, but on the English language, whose pronouns offer little help for the writer who wants to avoid sexist language.

I have adopted a similar compromise in choosing names for different stages of a child's growth. Various professional and academic groups use terms such as 'infant' and 'child' in a very precise way, but I have opted for common usage: 'infant' to mean a baby, and 'child' for all stages past the toddler stage, with 'teenager', 'early teens' and 'puberty' all having their commonly-accepted meanings.

In the same way, I have used the word 'play' throughout in a very general sense, to mean that part of a child's life which is recreational. This is because, of the two aspects of play—*how* children play, and *what* they play with—this book's emphasis is on the latter. For the same reason, there is comparatively little discussion of group games and team activities, and most of the book deals with toys and games, either played with in groups or by the child alone.

I

Some Early Play Experiences

What a large place to be small in
and what strange rooms—
how strong these arms; this shoulder
there when needed...
What a big world to be born into!
And full of things
I can't put names to; shapes
fearful and exciting, objects
that are removed from my grasp.
Later,
I will find them and know them. Meanwhile,
I am thirsty for milk,
my eyes are full of sleep.

David Porter[1]

Let us begin with the question: What are the things that influence children?

You don't have to spend very long with a child before you become aware that the first answer to this question is a very obvious one. The strongest influence on a child is—everything!

It's a simple point. It might be regarded as a simplistic one. But it's an important starting place in our thinking. Every experience, every fact learned, every opinion overheard, contributes to a child's increasing store of learned information, giving depth and meaning to its knowledge of the world.

Some students of childhood have taken this simple fact and derived sophisticated theories of development from it.

It's been a major factor, for example, in contemporary study of how we learn to talk; and some of the more extreme psychologists, following the lead of the behaviourist school, have suggested that any child can be made into any kind of individual, even against its will, if it is exposed to the right influences early enough. (It should be emphasised that today, very few professional psychologists believe this, though several futuristic science-fiction novels have used the notion with spectacular success.)

I sometimes wonder how much practical knowledge of children some of those celebrated psychologists possessed. Most parents and teachers know well enough that the learning process never finishes, that the child's development[2] is influenced as much in its school days as in its pre-school days, and that the learning process itself is much more complex than 'extreme behaviourism' would imply.

But you don't have to subscribe to an extreme view of childhood conditioning to acknowledge that a child's knowledge of the world develops gradually. There are many blanks to be filled in; there is much to be learned about people and about the world. That knowledge comes over a period of time.

And in that learning process, play matters.

Babies playing

Take for example the very first days and weeks of life. A very young baby is negotiating a world in which virtually nothing is known or understood. It is aware of the presence of its mother—though it will be a while before it sees her as anything more unique than a friendly, comforting shape and embracing arms—and of other people whose voices and physical identity it will gradually come to recognise. And it is vaguely aware of certain fixed points of time and geography in its world.

Does this mean that a child is a blank sheet of paper—a *tabula rasa*, a slate wiped clean on which anything can be written? That was what an earlier generation of thinkers believed. But 'the tradition...seldom considered the nature of the child as a child,' as the literary critic Peter Coveney has pointed out,[3] and today there is a common agreement that a baby brings into the world something significant of its own; whether it be merely hereditary characteristics, or—as the linguist Noam Chomsky, for example, would seem to suggest—the characteristics which belong to a baby simply by virtue of its *being* a human baby (a suggestion which should be particularly intriguing to Christians).

Our relationship to very young children has to keep in balance two things. One is that the baby in the crib is already a person with a personality, even though we may not be able to recognise very much of it at first (but how quickly that will change once the baby beings to smile and interrelate with its parents!). The other is that though the baby does not enter the world with nothing, it does enter it with very little. It is dependent, for enlarging its knowledge of how things are, on resources it is given to explore and on things that happen to it. So it is open and vulnerable, not only to physical danger but also to pressures on its developing mind and imagination.

Initiative and response

Even in those very early days of life, play performs a very important function.

Think of any baby, of two or three months or older, that you have recently seen lying in a pram. If it was awake, it was probably spending much of its time looking at, or playing with, toys that had been put in its pram—such as mobiles, beads that could be pushed along a cord, things that spun round when a small finger tapped them. At intervals, the baby's mother or other adults almost certainly appeared and attempted to attract the child's attention.

Adults looking at babies are actually important factors in the way a child learns the beginnings of social interaction. Communication is taking place, even if at first it is mainly a matter of the baby learning which facial expressions and gestures provoke pleased and happy responses from its audience.[4]

If a baby were to be left unattended in a pram for several hours—ignored completely by its parents, with nobody to answer its crying or to respond to its chuckles and gestures—most people would think it very cruel behaviour on the part of those who were supposed to be looking after him. Apart from the fact that its physical needs were not being met, most of us would point out that a baby needs human contact, that the mutual admiration between mother and child is vital for a child's development in a number of ways. A neglected baby is a stunted baby.

But what if the parents failed to provide any toys in the pram? If there were no rattles, threaded beads, or other objects to be played with?

Probably most people would not immediately see the absence of toys as damaging to the baby. After all, it is now well known that babies derive great pleasure from looking at things like patterned wallpaper and from tugging their own garments.[5] Passers-by would see the child following visual stimuli, turning its head to look at movement, or perhaps to locate an unfamiliar sound, and they would probably not consider it as being particularly deprived.

But in fact a baby without toys in its cot or pram *is* deprived of a number of important aids to development. It is deprived, for instance, of the discovery that certain move-ments have specific results. Dorothy Einon has described the 'great moment' when a child first touches a toy and sees it move: 'For the first time, he will have done something without your help.'[6] Similarly, reaching out for toys—another milestone—helps physical co-ordination. Simple cot and pram toys are often the result of extensive research into the acquisition of skills and co-ordination.

Thus, even at a very early age, play contributes a formative ingredient to a child's development. 'Not even in the first four months,' says Catherine Garvey, 'does an infant receive playful attention *passively*.'[7] But even left on his own, a child playing with toys, objects or even his own clothes and bedding is engaged in getting to know the world. Playing is a way of reaching into the large new world that surrounds it, and finding out what things feel, sound, smell, look and taste like.

> In the average good experience...the baby finds intense, even agonising pleasure associated with imaginative play. There is no set game, so everything is creative, and although playing is part of object-relating, whatever happens is personal to the baby. Everything physical is imaginately elaborated, is invested with a first-time-ever quality.[8]

Types of play

Let us move forward several years to late preschool age. The baby is now a child, and play is fulfilling an increasing number of functions. Toys are helping to develop visual and manipulative skills; for example, endless posting of geometrically shaped blocks into appropriate slots in a plastic letterbox is teaching very little about the postal service but an enormous amount about colour, size, shape, and how to tell different objects apart.

Whole new worlds of play are opening up, touching every area of personality and experience. Writers on the subject usually identify four broad types: social play, creative play, fantasy play and physical play. Not all these types of play are equally important to every age of child, but writing on *Play*

With a Purpose for Under-Sevens,[9] Elizabeth Matterson is able to devote whole chapters to adventure play, creative play, developing manipulative skill and co-ordination, music, books, story telling, pets and gardens, children confined to bed, and planning a playgroup—all of which are seen to be important and necessary for development.

By the preschool years, a child has also begun to develop imaginative fantasy play, where the imagination is contributing as much to the play experience as the physical characteristics of the object being played with—and of course, often the best fantasy play doesn't need toys at all. A paper bag, an arrangement of kitchen chairs, indeed anything that is handy and serves as a basis to build fantasy on will do. Our younger daughter, at the age of five, played for over an hour at 'being on television'—she made a large hole in the bottom of a cardboard box, drew simple knobs and buttons round the hole, clambered inside the box and proceeded to sing, talk and improvise for anybody who cared to stop and applaud.

The immediate preschool years are a time when children begin to derive great pleasure from playing with replicas and imitations of items from the adult world—a girl will play with toy tea-sets, for example, or a boy will pretend to drive a train (or the roles may be reversed, and there is no reason at all why that should cause alarm!).

But even from early infancy, the imagination is active in play, and some simple traditional games are teaching children important lessons. The game of 'let's pretend' is a natural extension of games like 'peek-a-boo', in which the child learns for the first time that people and objects continue to exist when they are no longer within one's field of view.

Games of fantasy and imagination, in which a child will create entire imaginary play countries and play companions, can absorb children of this age for whole days and even longer, and simple objects can be transformed into fascinating playthings rich with meanings with which the child has invested them. Many parents have had the experience of seeing a child at Christmas or a birthday, surrounded by expensive and educational presents, playing happily with the packaging in which they were wrapped; or the joy that can be gained from a cardboard box with a hole for a door and another for a window—especially if the child has helped to make those holes itself.

A loss of innocence

With the massive increase in external influences that comes with a child's first exposure to school (and to a lesser extent with its first involvement with playschool, though the absence of older children and various elements of primary school reduces the impact), children have to readjust their perceptions of how the world operates.

One common phenomenon of these years, for example, is a change in the child's relationship to television. In infancy, a baby simply sees shapes on screen and does not 'read' them in terms of its own felt and perceived world. Later, it identifies faces as belonging to people, even though those people's bodies may not be visible on screen. Elements of recognition begin to appear; a child will recognise, and attempt to greet, a familiar face on television.[10]

The end of the process that starts when a child realises that television images *are* mere images and not objects inside the box comes with the realisation that though the fictions *are* fictions, they nevertheless portray events that could actually happen.

Which is why a child can become very agitated on seeing, for example, a transparently contrived death of a pet animal on television. 'I know it's only pretend,' sobbed my daughter on one such occasion. 'But it *could* happen. It could happen to Bilbo,' she added, clutching our much-loved family cat.

It's a kind of loss of innocence.

A similar experience of early school days is the discovery that books are not infallible. Children acquire a great deal of information from books, about places and events of which they are not themselves able to be witnesses. But I well remember the shock of disillusionment experienced by my older daughter when, at the age of seven or eight, she sat with me and showed me a library book about dinosaurs (every child seems to go through a fascination-with-dinosaurs phase, and I don't think that psychologists know why!). Pointing to a brontosaurus, she showed me the splendid green armour with which the artist had endowed it. The book was a particularly garish one, and I didn't like it very much, and I didn't see why my daughter should be conditioned by that fairly mediocre artist. So I gently suggested that the green colouring was just the artist's guess, and reminded her that only the bones survive.

'Oh no,' she explained. 'Dinosaurs are *green*. See, it shows you in this book.'

She would have been unmovable, but I happened to find another illustrated book on dinosaurs.

'Look,' I said. 'Dark brown.'

The expression on her face signified a small loss of faith; a landmark in her private world had disappeared. Things in books were no longer true just because they were in books.

Parental roles

I am not attempting to write a chronological study of children and play—which has been done very well by a number of other authors—but I want to identify, at the beginning of this book, one or two characteristics of a child's experience of play at an early age.

Firstly, *children at play are not just whiling away time*, or merely using their bodies. They are engaged with their whole beings, and therefore the things that they play with will in some way or other, to a tiny or a substantial extent, have some part in forming the kind of people they become and the way they think about the world and about themselves. Their evolving experience of play is, in a real sense, an evolving experience of the world in which they are going to live.

Secondly, *children are vulnerable*. The toys they are provided with have the capability of reinforcing their world, or threatening it. In their play, they can be helped or hindered by the resources they are given. For example, the baby in the pram needs toys; care spent in providing good-quality toys that are designed to develop skills and perceptions will be reflected in a better-adjusted, even happier child.

Thirdly, *play involves adults*. Caring for children, whether it be as parent, teacher or in some other relationship, should mean caring for them when they are at play just as much as when they are at work. If we treat play as a means of keeping the children quiet, and heave a sigh of relief whenever they become absorbed in a toy or a game—because now we can get on with other things—we are missing a great opportunity to involve ourselves in our children's development at a very creative level.

It's important to keep a balance between taking an interest in your child's play, and monopolising it! It can be agonisingly frustrating to watch a child with a new toy, struggling to master some detail of unpacking or basic operation, when you are longing to see the child playing with it as the designers intended and as you intended when you bought the toy. But experimentation and learning are important for the child, and if you step in and do the work for them, you are depriving them of something that would help them.

But a well-judged involvement with children's play is important, because the child needs adult help to deal with the self-discovery that play brings with it.

Play...has infinite possibility in it. It enables the child to experience whatever is to be found in his or her personal inner psychic reality, which is the basis of the growing sense of reality. There will be aggression there as well as love.[11]

Most parents will have had the experience of seeing a child locked in a tantrum, clearly wanting to calm down but not knowing how to; or one appalled at having been aggressive towards a small friend and not really knowing why. Play can often arouse such emotions, and children are not always able to handle them. At play, they are discovering themselves and their friends in a way that they will not do through more formal learning processes. Abandoning them to their own devices is deprivation, whether it happens by neglect, thoughtlessness, or simply the numerous demands that there are on most parents' and teachers' time.

These three characteristics of the child's mind—its openness, its tendency to trust (and sometimes be disappointed) and the need for adult interest—may seem obvious and hardly worth devoting a whole chapter to. But they are characteristics which underlie all the topics to be covered in this book.

Play often has the effect of defining the child's world. For example, we'll be looking at the issue of violent toys later. It's a complex issue. It is much too easy to assume that all symbols of violence and aggression, and all aggressive games, are equally and identically harmful to children; for some children it may well be that playing with toy guns is a positive and therapeutic exercise.

For some children and in some circumstances, the game with the gun may be quite acceptable. For others, it may well fuel existing aggressions or create new ones. There are other dimensions to the problem; for example, there are often unacceptable political models implicit in some packaging of war toys. And we will be looking at those issues in a later chapter.

But in the present context I want to emphasise that the decision process can't be sidestepped. We need to acknowledge that some children may be imaginatively harmed by such playing, and assess whether a particular child will benefit from it or not. Whether it's a major family crisis-decision, or just a parent making a snap decision in the light of what is known about the child and the game or toy in question, responsible child care, whether in home or play-ground, will involve making some sort of choice.

And choices bring with them obligations. The vulnerability of the growing child means that caring for children at play is a *responsibility*. That applies not just to parents, but to anybody who works with, or is in some other way involved with, children.

Protection and preparation

Some readers of *Children at Risk* suggested that what was being recommended in that book was an unrealistic and not very helpful idealism; that one couldn't watch children every hour of the day, and that it was not in their interests to do so anyway.

I agree with their concerns, but I don't think it is idealistic to talk about protecting children—provided, that is, that we also talk about *preparing* them. The task of caring for children involves sheltering them from a world that is full of risks and pressures, while at the same time preparing them to live in that world.

It means choosing the right time for a child to move on to the next stage. It may, for example, mean the kind of decision that I and my wife are faced with, living in a small village on a busy road—when do we allow our children to walk home from school unattended, or to cycle on the main road? It may be a decision about whether or not to allow a child to play with violent toys or to read violent books. It will certainly be a choice that will have a part to play in the development of the child.

It's a choice that can only be properly exercised when we are aware of how prone the child is to be affected and influenced by any part of its environment. Parents in particular know how amazingly open the child's mind is.

Memory is a good example.

You don't have to be into middle age to have problems remembering things. Very few adults have the ability to keep facts in mind over a long period without using some technique or trick to help them do so—which is why books on new methods of developing a 'good memory' sell so well!

Yet I am often astonished at the capacity of my own children to remember tiny details of things I'd long ago forgotten. They will pick up some trinket and remember exactly where it came from, or tell me about books they read when they were much younger.

The reason is, of course, that children's memories are less crammed than ours. Less has happened to them; there is less to be remembered. I know quite a few lengthy poems by heart; but I learned almost all of them when I was quite young. When I try to memorise a poem today, it has to be fitted in among all the accumulated bits and pieces of memories of all the years I've lived, things I've seen and things I've done. And there simply isn't as much room as there is in my five-year-old daughter's memory.

In the same way, young children haven't developed barriers against shock or fear in the way that adults have. Often play can present them with personal discoveries or even personal crises with which they cannot cope unaided.

What influences a child's mind? Everything. A caring adult will want to ensure that as much of the child's life as possible is brought within the umbrella of parenthood, or teaching, or any other adult-child relationship. And that includes play.

This doesn't mean that an adult has to direct a child's play, or become a child in order to play with one. Nor does it mean that playing with children can be consigned to the category of necessary evils.

Certainly parents are happy to see their children absorbed in play. But are they equally happy to become engrossed in the playing themselves? If a child's play is pleasurable to a parent chiefly because he can then pursue his adult activities without neglecting his child, it does not take the child long to realize this.... The true test of a parent's belief about play is reflected not in what he says, but in how he behaves.[12]

Play is enjoyable to children, and it's an enjoyment that adults can share. In the early years, it can strengthen immeasurably the bonding between child and parent. In early childhood, it can contribute to the learning process and give strong support to the emerging, developing personality of the child. In later childhood, adults who can share the imaginative world of play with children will find that their relationships with those children are deeper, more understanding, and more binding.

A play-community generally tends to become permanent even after the game is over.... The feeling of being 'apart together' in an exceptional situation, of sharing something important, of mutually withdrawing from the rest of the world and rejecting the usual norms, retains its magic beyond the duration of the individual game.[13]

To be with a child at play is more than a useful way of discharging parental responsibilities. It is to know the child in a unique way.

2

Heroes and Role Models

"Well, Zerelda, I can't have you in my class like this," she said, looking very prim and bird-like. "Take down that roll of hair. Tie it all back. Clean your lips. Come back to the room in five minutes." And with that she disappeared into the form room and the door was shut.

Zerelda stared after her. She patted the roll of hair on top. What was the matter with her? Didn't it make her look exactly like Lossie Laxton, the film star she admired most of all?

Zerelda frowned. What a school! Here were a whole lot of girls, all growing up fast, and not one of them knew how to do her hair.

Enid Blyton[1]

In the previous chapter we looked at a very simple aspect of the child's imaginative and play life: its whole environment. In this chapter we will be looking at something that is just as generalised among children and teenagers: the need to possess heroes and role models.

As a starting point, however, we should consider something which is even more central to the child's development.

Peer-group pressure

It's a natural instinct of childhood to want to belong to a group, and it's much more than just a herd instinct. Whether in playgroup gangs, 'best friends', or—most noticeably, as

problems of self-esteem and pressure to achieve start to
emerge—teenage circles, a child can be part of a social
grouping that is not his family (thereby gaining indepen-
dence) and be distinguished from the rest of his contemporaries by virtue of his membership of the group (thereby
gaining status).

Samantha, aged five or six, was having an earnest conversation with another girl of the same age. They were cat-
egorising their schoolfriends into two groups: those who
liked playing with Barbie dolls, and those who liked playing
with Sindy dolls. They themselves were in the Sindy doll
group, and they poured scorn on those who liked Barbie
dolls, listing all the reasons why Barbie dolls were toys for
kids, while Sindy dolls were a quite different matter. The
girls were identifying themselves as part of a *group*.

> Teenagers have found a corporate entity and a self-conscious
> awareness of being in a class of their own: neither child nor
> adult.... The characteristics which open up the way to peer-
> group pressure are present even in the very young. Junior school
> children who have recently left the tolerant and kindly ethos of
> their infant classroom are...easily hurt by any form of rejection
> by their friends. They often have a great need to identify with
> their own age group.[2]

As children enter the teenage years and begin to become
more interested in possessions and the implications that possessions have for status, peer group pressure can again be
strong. For example, bitter arguments rage in the correspondence columns of many computer magazines as the rival
merits of the Commodore Amiga and the Atari ST computers (two very similar machines) are debated, as are those
of the Commodore 64 and the Sinclair Spectrum machines.
Many of the letters come from teenagers, and often sound
reminiscent of the Barbie/Sindy conversation quoted earlier!

School stories have traditionally made peer-group acceptance an important part of adolescent life. The desire to be

accepted, and more particularly to be on the inside, is for
example a common theme in Enid Blyton's school stories:

> The whole form was in a state of excitement that day. It was
> simply gorgeous to have a secret and not to let any of the other
> forms know. Hilary knew that the upper third had had a mid-
> night feast already that term, and it had been a great success.
> She meant to make theirs even more of a success![3]

C. S. Lewis describes the urge well in an address given in
1944:

> I believe that in all men's lives at certain periods, and in many
> men's lives at all periods between infancy and extreme old age,
> one of the most dominant elements is the desire to be inside the
> local Ring and the terror of being left outside.[4]

Imitating one's peers

Along with the desire to be part of a group comes the urge to
imitate other children.

Anyone who has watched children of any age at play will
have observed how ready they are to imitate others. I think
that there are two reasons why this is so.

One is the desire to reinforce the membership of the peer
group; to look the same as everybody else. I was told of a
boy who, when his friends were due to visit, would wait by
his bedroom window to see them coming down the road. If
they were in long trousers and he was in shorts, he would
change into long trousers and be waiting ready for them
when they arrived; and vice versa. He couldn't bear to stand
out from the crowd, and anybody who has accidentally
bought a child the wrong item of school uniform will know
how important conformity is to children.

By imitation, children gain a sense of group identity.
Whether it's a desire to wear what is currently fashionable,
or to be doing what everybody else is doing—coupled with a
dread of being the odd one out, the only one who isn't

wearing plaits or playing He-Man games—the urge to conform, to imitate one's peers, is very strong.

The second reason for imitation is that it's a part of the
learning process. The child is growing into a world that is
new, strange, and often disturbing, and so looks, for an
example, to those who seem to be negotiating that confusing
world better than they are themselves.

Thus children will often imitate people whom they reckon
to be their betters. It may be as simple as copying the
personal mannerisms of an elder brother or sister, in an
attempt to acquire the poise and confidence which the younger child, perhaps optimistically, perceives in the older.
Most children, too, go through a phase of imitating their
parents. Some become frustrated because they are unsuc-
cessfully trying to become like their schoolteacher, or their
Sunday School superintendent, or any other adult who
seems to be the kind of adult that the child wants to, and
believes he might, become. In some cases it will develop into
a crush on a teacher or another adult. In every case there will
be some attempt to wear the same clothes, adopt the same
mannerisms, speak with the same accent, or in some other
way to make the child's own life resemble that of the person
who is admired.

Heroes and role models

What I have been describing is the process of acquiring a role
model. The child, entering unfamiliar territory, watches the
'natives' to find out the best way to get through, and not
unnaturally chooses to copy those natives who seem to be
getting through with the most flair and ease. It is part of the
inexorable logic of childhood.

Children acquire their *heroes*, however, by a similar, yet
essentially different, process. A hero is somebody who lives
on a higher plane than his or her admirer.

Pop fashions

An obvious example is pop music, which has always provided heroes for young people. For many people, a rock star is what they would like to be. But relatively few children actually play or sing rock music, and not many actively strive to excel in music so that they can aspire to star status themselves.

Contemporary idols of the popular music scene often deliver opinions on all sorts of subjects that have nothing to do with pop music. Sometimes there are problems when a hero falls from grace, as for example when Boy George was the subject of massive media coverage because of his involvement with drugs. He had previously appeared on television chat shows projecting a thoughtful, responsible image rather at odds with his bizarre appearance. After the drugs exposure he had to rebuild his reputation not so much as a musician but as a hero, and today he frequently advises young people to have nothing to do with drugs (though his public statements on sexuality are as unorthodox and ambiguous as they have ever been).

Heroes of the pop world today are often tarnished heroes; for example, many have disastrous and widely publicised relationship problems. But that hardly matters in the fast-moving world of pop culture, which thrives on change, instant obsolescence and topical rather than abiding values.

Style

In the 1960s hair fashions were an obvious indicator of who the pop heroes were, as teenagers began to acquire mop-head haircuts. Today fashions are just as much influenced by the current leaders of the pop world, as for example when Madonna's success made bare midriffs popular.

It's important, too, to know the *latest* trends, what's in and what's out. To have street-credibility, the older child needs to know that there are certain music groups that people aren't listening to any more, that a particular alternative comedian is currently much admired, and whatever other topical style trends there may be.

As I write, Filofaxes are becoming trendy among older teenagers, possibly due to a combination of the fact that a character in television's *Eastenders* carries one prominently, and the fact that a major bank is offering free Filofaxes to young people opening accounts.

Not so long ago, rap poetry—fast talking, rhythmic, poetry originating in the black community—dominated, and the latest craze was body-popping break-dancing. Now house music (high-tech, high volume dance music) is currently fashionable. By the time that this book is published, everything will have moved on. Young people will be preoccupied with something different.

The meeting of worlds

One of the most dreamed-of fantasies among people who have personal heroes is to meet that hero in the flesh—even more, to know him or her as a personal friend. It's true that most people would readily agree that a hero who became your best friend would probably cease to be a hero in the same way. Nevertheless, there's an insatiable curiosity about the hero's likes and dislikes, family details, and any minute pieces of information that can be obtained.

The magazines which are published for children and teenagers play heavily on this fantasy. In *Number One*, for example, a double-page feature offered '50 absolutely staggering things you didn't know about the Pet Shop Boys!' Here are a few taken at random:

   1. Chris can play the trombone.
 13. The Petshop Boys were at the opening of the Wacko Jacko film *Captain Eo* in Disneyland.
 17. Neil goes jogging. Chris prefers to work-out in a gym.

26. They once appeared in a TV advert in Japan for Maxell tapes.
41. Neil is quite obsessed with cashpoints. His flat is even over one![5]

Of course there is an element of humour here. But there is also the offer of intimate details about the stars, the opportunity to reach a little way behind the mask and the public image, and discover the kind of things that their personal friends and acquaintances know about them. (The fact that many features of this kind are dreamed up by the journalists or music agents, and many of the 'facts' are quite fictitious, doesn't matter in the least.)

For some lucky young people, the chance to meet the star in person is offered. 'A night out with Nick!' boasted the cover of *My-Guy* magazine, a magazine for older teenagers, and explains in a colour feature inside:

> "...!" That's just about all reader Karen Murphy could manage to splutter when we told her she'd won a night out on the town with the *extremely* yumlicious Nick Heyward.[6]

The photographs accompanying the story show a very relaxed star ('The cheekiest cheesy grin in pop') and a pleasant, ordinary and apparently quite nervous young lady, photographed in a fashionable London restaurant. The fact that Karen drank only soft drinks, and her mother was present, deglamourised the situation effectively—there was never any possibility that Karen was going to become a pop star herself; but the title of the story ('Brief Encounter') evoked a quite different aura for the evening. 'Sweet dreams for the young Karen Murphy,' concluded the journalist who was writing the whole thing up. 'Somehow, life'll never be the same again.'

In stories like this two worlds collide: the world of the glamorous pop stars, who live in exotic restaurants where everybody is extremely yumlicious; and the world of Karen and her Mum, who choose 'fish 'n' chips with a posh name' at the restaurant and arrive on the InterCity 125 from Basingstoke....

Photo-stories

The colliding worlds of glamour and ordinary life are the theme behind a type of story which has become very common in girl's magazines: the photo story. It works by using real-life black-and-white photographs to tell a story in a series of frames, like a strip-cartoon except that the characters are real people. Their thoughts and what they say appear in speech balloons drawn in over the photographs.

An example appears in *Girl*, in the issue of 9 April 1988. The plot runs as follows. Karen (a popular name in the magazines) is rushing for her school bus. She is dressed in school clothes, and is obviously intended to look like a typical schoolgirl. At the bus-stop a strange old lady offers her a banana, which she declines. When the bus arrives, it is half empty, but the old lady insists on sitting next to her and continues to talk very oddly about bananas.

'If only someone would help me!' she thinks, and in the photograph you can see an attractive young man, wearing a fashionable and expensive-looking leather jacket. He comes over to her and asks if she would like to sit with him. She accepts gratefully. He introduces himself. They chat, and she is greatly relieved to be free of the strange old lady, now sitting on her own behind them.

They reach her stop; it is the young man's as well. As they get off the bus, the old lady does so too. She summons the young man to her, much to Karen's alarm. 'I'm not afraid of her bananas,' smiles the boy. Incredulously, she sees the old lady kiss him affectionately. 'I hope that was all right, love, I'll see you later at your Mum's.'

'Okay. Thanks, Gran,' replies the boy, and the revelation follows that he had persuaded his grandmother to play the part, because he had seen Karen several times on the bus and wanted to ask her out. And the story ends with the two all set for a ripening friendship.

How the stories work

This story has several elements which are common in magazine stories (and not only those for young people; magazines for adults often use the same devices). Firstly, there is the arrival of a glamorous, handsome, attractively dressed figure into the everyday world of the central character. Secondly, there is the obstacle to their meeting. Thirdly, the off-beat device of the banana-woman, itself the kind of crazy, fun idea that belongs to a different world than the boring school bus and the shapeless school pullover.

And yet the handsome stranger fell in love with her while she was on the bus, wearing the school uniform. In stories like these, the glamorous stranger or the star falls for the heroine *because she is ordinary*. So the reader can fantasise that it could happen to her as well; she doesn't have to turn herself into a star or a glamorous person herself, because she is just like the person in the story—and what happened to the girl in the story could therefore quite possibly happen to her as well!

Television as a role model

Girls' magazines are just one of many ways in which the child's developing imagination and play-world are offered examples to imitate and heroes to follow.

One very strong influence is television. The 'effects debate' is a complex one, and in several areas it is unresolved. Yet there are some assumptions that can, I think, be made with reasonable confidence. One assumption is that if children watch television regularly, some of the attitudes, information and values of the programmes they see will become part of the way that they look at life.

An example is the Australian soap opera *Neighbours*, which has acquired an audience including an enormous number of children, following a deliberate change of marketing policy giving high profile to storylines about school, romances between children in their early teens, a marriage between two teenagers, and other storylines featuring young people (although an attractive aspect of the story is that middle-aged and older people are also shown as having a rich life; in *Neighbours*, falling in love and enjoying life aren't just something for young people).

Neighbours is transmitted twice a day, every weekday. Children who watch tend to watch the evening repeat, which falls neatly into the slot once occupied by 'Children's Hour', and now acknowledged to be a time when children's interests will be catered for. It is quite addictive, and there is considerable peer-group pressure to be up-to-date with the latest events.

When a child is watching something regularly, at a fixed time every day, it might be assumed that it would have some influence on the choices the child makes. From my own observation of children who watch *Neighbours*, here are some of the influences which I have noticed children responding to:

(a) In the programme, people constantly apologise to each other when they have offended, inconvenienced or harmed them. Some children have, through *Neighbours*, come to see this as important in their own relationships.

(b) Unlike many foreign soaps and sit-coms, the children in *Neighbours* are not there to display their superior cuteness and outwit the older generation. People talk to each other, and the generations communicate. The three-tier family is accepted and valued. *Neighbours* certainly has the possibility of helping children relate to their older relations.

(c) Kylie Minogue, who plays Charlene, is a major celebrity in the pop world as well as an actor in the programme. She is very much a heroine for many children. The things they admire about her *Neighbours* character include her determination to succeed in a male-dominated industry (car maintenance), her insistence that having married young, she and her husband Scott are not going to be a drain on others' resources, her loyalty to her husband and the fact that she was willing to sell her wedding dress to help Scott's career as a journalist, and her loyalty to her family in the face of an extraordinary series of catastrophes and setbacks.

These are just three of the ways that *Neighbours* can influence its young audience, and I think they are all of value.

That's not to say that in many ways it isn't an appallingly unrealistic, technically patchy and dreadfully simplistic soap opera (for example, no crisis seems to last for more than two or three episodes, including Lucy's brain tumour and the theft of Helen Daniels' priceless paintings!). And of course there are many other issues surrounding soap opera, and some give many parents good cause for concern.[7] Television soap opera can be extremely addictive, for example, both for young and old. I was told recently of a seven-year-old who dissolved into tears and threw an enormous tantrum when visiting a friend of mine—all because she did not allow him to watch the lunchtime episode of *Neighbours*.

But there are some positive influences as well, and provided that other risks are properly taken into consideration, I personally have no problem in allowing my children to watch *Neighbours* (though for various reasons, they actually see it fairly infrequently).

A very different soap opera is *Eastenders*. This also goes out relatively early in the evening—7.30 pm—twice a week, and the Sunday omnibus edition is transmitted between 2 and 3 pm in the afternoon. Like *Neighbours*, it deals with a close-knit community, this time in the East End of London. It is a more sophisticated product than *Neighbours*: better written, often better acted, and better produced and directed.

Where *Neighbours* has one or two broadly-sketched family units, with clearly defined relationships between families and a common commitment to neighbourhood unity, the families in *Eastenders* are lined up on opposing sides of a number of complex family wars. The older people in *Neighbours* are simply drawn, usually patriarchal and matriarchal figures who dispense wisdom and counsel while remaining full of life and creativity themselves (the major exception, Mrs Mangel, only serves to emphasise the cartoon-strip nature of much of the programme). In *Eastenders*, age does not necessarily bring wisdom, nor does it always bring respect and family devotion.

As a result, the influences of the programme are more subtle and sophisticated. A child who is influenced by the behaviour of a character in *Neighbours* is influenced because his or her better nature is being appealed to: the character points to some generally accepted standard of morality or ethics, and the viewer either agrees or disagrees. In *Eastenders*, it is the character who is compelling, so that a child who admires and respects a character such as Michelle will tend to respect the decisions that character makes, even though the character will often confess that he or she does not know absolutely whether their course of action is the 'right' one—as for example when Michelle aborted her child against the wishes of its father.

Given that the child's developing imagination is open to influence, the influences coming from television are sometimes relatively simple and straightforward, and sometimes complex and difficult to identify.

Other heroes and role models

There are many more role models available to children. One, for example, is sports personalities. Many are from disadvantaged backgrounds, and many from minority groups, and children in those minorities naturally admire and respect achievers who have overcome the difficulties they face themselves.

Playground play is often modelled on sports figures, particularly when sport is in the news, for example during the Olympic Games or the World Cup. When Japanese Sumo wrestling became a cult Channel 4 series, skinny youngsters could be seen emulating the feats of the thirty-stone Sumo giants.

Sports heroes have always been a feature of the child's world, and there have been many portrayals of the sportsman or sportswoman as hero—for example, the film *Chariots of Fire*. Not many people would deny that the values of competitive sport are often fine ones for children to prize: the importance of team work, the necessity for physical fitness, the value of single-minded pursuit of achievement.

It's interesting, however, to find that sports stars have often acquired the same type of glamour that pop stars possess. On the cover of *Blue Jeans*, for example, when the Coe/Ovett/Cram rivalry was at its height, athletics heroes were featured in the same large type as TV stars: 'COMMONWEALTH GAMES—Seb Coe, Steve Cram and Daley Thompson in dinky little shorts. Need we say more?'[8]

Sports figures go in and out of fashion, and few have survived as popular heroes for long periods. But that is how the glamorising effect of the pop culture works.

The adult's response

What should the response of parents and teachers be to the hero-worship phenomenon?

Firstly, *we must recognise its existence*. This is often more easily said than done. It is possible to imagine that the influences do not exist when in fact they are very strong. For example, parents who do not possess a television might think that their children are not affected by television at all, unaware of the access they have through friends, and teachers who think that their school community is remarkably free of comics and magazines might be surprised to see the posters pinned up on the bedroom walls of their pupils.

Not long ago I was giving a talk to a mixed group of adults and young people, on the subject of television soap opera. It's a subject I've studied in some depth, and I talked for some time, showing video clips and demonstrating how soap operas communicate to us on many levels, not all of which we recognise.[9]

When I had finished I asked for questions, and a man rose to his feet and thanked me for the talk I had given. It was very helpful, he said, to be made aware of how television affects us, but for him personally and his family it was a purely academic issue. They did not own a television, he said, and so his children didn't have the problem.

Later in the discussion, a fifteen-year-old girl began to ask some detailed questions. She knew a great deal about soap opera, and cross-examined me on plots, issues and other specialised topics. When she sat down, I realised I had had my credibility checked out by an expert.

It was only afterwards, chatting socially over coffee, that I discovered that the teenager was the daughter of the man who had asked the first question.

Secondly, *we must listen to our children*. They live in a world which has its own ever-changing language and reference points. It's not enough to know what was popular a year ago. Caring for children involves constantly keeping one ear open to the contemporary fashions, phrases and attitudes that are current now.

Sometimes we miss valuable opportunities for communication.

The large church was packed for a family service. There were about two dozen teenagers in the congregation. The preacher was talking about modern materialism—how we are becoming more and more obsessed with the desire to own things, to have possessions, to acquire an image: in short, to have enormous quantities of money.

He warmed to his theme, and quoted from the Old and New Testaments. He told some good jokes. He even drew illustrations from contemporary culture. And slowly but surely, the teenagers fell asleep.

The irony was that he could have secured their attention by saying a single word. That word would have been incomprehensible to most of his adult listeners, but to most kids at that time it was part of their everyday vocabulary. The word was 'loadsamoney'.

It's a catchword, used by a character from the evening TV show *Saturday Night Live* on Channel 4. Loadsamoney was a character created by comedian Harry Enfield, and was an appallingly uncouth, very loud, very rich builder who taunted his audience with wads of banknotes, shouting 'Loadsamoney! Loadsamoney!'

At the time of the family service, every kid on the block could do a Loadsamoney impersonation, and words like 'loadsafun', 'loadsamusic' and so on were being used on every side. Before then, the fashionable word was 'mega', but now nobody with street credibility said it any more....

Eavesdropping after hours

In fact, the popularity of Loadsamoney raises several issues that are very relevant to our discussion.

For example, *Saturday Night Live* was broadcast late in the evening. And even if we accept that quite a number of children make unauthorised after-hours use of their parents' video recorders (one reason, incidentally, why even late-night TV must not be left without controls and guidelines); and if we also accept that there are many children who have no idea that *Saturday Night Live* exists—the amount of informed mimicry by children of its two main stars, Ben Elton and Harry Enfield, still indicates that a substantial number of children were staying up. And that suggests that the IBA and BBC guidelines about 'family viewing hours' (assumed to end at 9 pm) cannot be taken as an easy solution to the problems of children and television, and parents must take their share of responsibility for control—something which, it should be emphasised, the broadcasting authorities have themselves been careful to advise.

Again, Enfield's character is a political satire. Loadsamoney is a criticism of the wealth-creating economy proposed by the Conservative government under Margaret Thatcher. Another Enfield character, Stavros the Greek, is an affectionate caricature of a Greek immigrant and a satire on British attitudes. Ben Elton is a very political comedian (and also one whose satire carries a strong note of moral anger). And in the programme as a whole, there are a number of underlying assumptions and attitudes that the comedy is reinforcing. The same is true of any comedy.

What ought to make parents and teachers pause to think is that numerous children can imitate Ben Elton, or Loadsamoney, or Stavros the Greek; political and other arguments that are completely acceptable for an older audience are being absorbed, incomplete and half-understood, by some quite young children.

Finally, *we must not rush to condemn hero worship and role modelling*. It can be a helpful phase. When I was at school I had a friend whom I admired greatly. He was a brighter student than I was, and occupied a higher position in the form than I did. Because I admired him and wanted to be like him, I worked harder and began to improve, particularly in English literature. Another schoolfriend, who went on to become an organ scholar at a very young age, introduced me to classical music. I knew very little about it, but because I wanted to be like him, I began to listen to the music and grew to love it. I owe both John Wallace and Andrew Beaizley a debt for introducing me to literature and music, both of which are extremely important to me as an adult.

It's important to look at the heroes and models our children follow, because even in the most unlikely ones what is being modelled to them may be helpful. The odd-looking hairstyle and weird slang phrases might not be the only things your child is taking on board. Of course, there will probably be good and bad influences mixed up together, and even if you decide that the helpful outweighs the unhelpful, the situation must be watched with care.

Conclusion

Of course, there are exceptions: children who doggedly go their own way, scorning the customs and loyalties of their peer groups, preserving an aloof individuality when their contemporaries are striving to be as like each other as possible. And there are also lonely children, trying to cope with an individuality they would rather exchange for being one of the crowd.

Yet the influence of role models and peer-group pressure remains strong even on those who do not, or cannot, follow the crowd. Peer-group pressure, particularly for an adolescent, is all the stronger a force if one is not part of the group. And the solitary child, isolated either by choice or by loneliness, is often following a private role model of his or her own.

So I would suggest that the themes we have been considering in this chapter establish some useful ground-rules for any thinking about influences on the imaginative life of children. We need to be aware that children are influenced, and we need to have some knowledge of what the things are that influence them. But we should be determined to avoid either blanket denunciation or blanket endorsement.

And we need to keep our own relationship with our

children constantly under review. The ultimate role models for children are often the adults closest to them.

Followers of many faiths share a common agenda so far as children are concerned. Jewish, Sikh, Islamic and many other families have a deep concern for the family and a desire to equip their children to lead fulfilled and worthwhile lives in the modern world. Those of us whose concern for our children grows out of our religious view of life must accept that parenthood and teaching are not responsibilities that can be discharged just by sitting back and letting the children get on with it.

If we are Christian parents, we will want our children to grow up into Christian men and women who will take Jesus as their model. But it is to us they will look to find that model presented to them. I find it encouraging that role models and heroes are endorsed in the Bible: for example, the apostle Paul—after a passage of great humility—invites his readers to take him as their model:

> Not that I have already obtained all this, or have already been made perfect, but I press on to take hold of that for which Christ Jesus took hold of me. Brothers, I do not consider myself yet to have taken hold of it. But one thing I do: forgetting what is behind and straining toward what is ahead, I press on toward the goal to win the prize for which God has called me heavenward in Christ Jesus.... Join with others in following my example, brothers, and take note of those who live according to the pattern we gave you.[10]

Paul is not being arrogant. He knows that he has taken as his own role model somebody whose example can be commended to everybody. Imitating Paul is therefore like imitating Jesus.

In these first two chapters, we have looked at the developing child and the environment in which play happens. In our next chapter, we will begin to look at the toys themselves.

3

A World Without Morals?

"What are you thinking about, Teddy Bear?"
"Nothing."

Aldous Huxley[1]

Michael is dressed in a cowboy outfit. He is sitting on an upturned bucket, staring into the distance. His mother calls him, but he doesn't hear her. He is chasing Indians in the Wild West.

Alison, aged four, is sitting on the settee, a dinner-plate held vertically by the rim in both hands, her brow furrowed in concentration as she turns the plate this way and that. She is driving Mummy's car along the road.

Charlie, out in the back garden, is wearing a balaclava helmet and holding a long stick. He is crawling on all fours in the garden, harpooning whales. His sister, curled up in front of the fire with a book, is adventuring in Middle Earth.

It's often been said that when children play, they enter into a world of their own. It is a world that is defined by what they play with. A toy pony, for example, can work the magic:

> Your own baby pony to adopt and care for—this beautiful Baby Pony is yours when you join our fabulous 1989 My Little Pony Activity Club.... You will become its Mummy and welcome it into your own Pony family.[2]

Reading this it is easy to smile, but it ought to be said that one of the great benefits of dolls, certainly for little girls, is that they are enabled to act out the mother-role, and that the toys often flesh out that role by providing details and characteristics of particular dolls to be mothered.

However, it might be argued that it's only when you have sophisticated toys like those we have today, and children who are exposed to the media, that the sort of language used in the advertisement quoted above is meaningful. But the author of *The Wind in the Willows*, remembering his own Victorian childhood, recalls the magic too, talking about a rocking horse:

> When the military spirit was abroad, who so ready to be a squadron of cavalry, a horde of Cossacks, or artillery pounding into position? He had even served with honour as a gun-boat, during a period when naval strategy was the only theme; and no false equine pride ever hindered him from taking the part of a roaring locomotive, earth-shaking, clangorous, annihilating time and space...[3]

Toys as we know them today are a comparatively recent innovation, and are the product of a number of historical factors, such as the expansion of industry in the nineteenth century and the corresponding rise of, for example, the tin toy.

> By the eighteen-nineties the development of offset lithography enabled complicated designs in full colour to be printed effortlessly on to thousands of sheets of tinplate which could then be cut and pressured into shape.[4]

The explosion of the rubber and plastics industries have obviously had a comparable effect in our own time.

And it was not until quite recent times that childhood was acknowledged as a unique phase of imaginative and spiritual growth, rather than simply a time when tiny adults-in-waiting grew bigger. Isaac Watts, writing for the managers of charity schools in 1728, strictly limited the play opportunities for children:

> For sports and diversions, draughts and chess are rather grudgingly allowed. Watts hesitates to condemn cards and dice so long as there is no gambling, but suggests that "little tablets of paste-board be made in imitation of cards, which might teach...grammar, philosophy...geography, etc." He would clearly have approved of jigsaw puzzles and such games as "Scrabble".[5]

Watts was writing in the tradition of the Puritans, who mistrusted the imagination and tried to harness it to spiritual applications. Clearly he was aware that toys and games have a power to influence children, and he was not willing to run the risk!

What sort of a world?

To play successfully with other people you have to accept rules, and rules imply a crude morality. Nothing destroys a play-world so completely as a spoilsport. And to believe in the world in which you are playing, you have to accept at least in part, and temporarily, the values of the world in which you play.

I'm not suggesting that this means that such play is harmful, but simply that it is not neutral. Even simple, disposable toys for solitary play carry some implications.

> The aims of toymakers in the late 19th and 20th centuries were much simpler than they are nowadays. Then you just made an amusing object which was in some way a comment on society.... One of the main qualities of the penny toy is its light social comment reflected in the choice of subject-matter.[6]

In the 1990s, the same is true. 'Tropical Barbie' places Barbie in an exotic playground, with a colourful swimsuit adorning her wasplike figure, and fashionable boxer shorts for her boyfriend Ken. The packaging makes a week at

Skegness in August look distinctly drab by comparison. A child playing with Tropical Barbie knows what a super holiday looks like.

Toys are rarely *criticisms* of society. They make comments by reinforcing values and suggesting targets for pleasure and achievement. In the world of Barbie, Hollywood glamour and a luxurious lifestyle are seen as things to be admired and fantasised about. Future social historians will learn as much about our society from such toys as we can learn today about Victorian society when we look at the toys they played with.

Toys and the world of the imagination

I want to suggest that the imaginative world of play that is promoted by much of today's toy industry and game industry, and the media, can actually be divided into two worlds, which overlap but broadly speaking represent two distinct focuses. The first is the world that I would call *the amoral fantasy world*, and the second I would call *the moral fantasy world*.

Let me say at once that these are not in themselves terms of criticism and endorsement, and I am not saying that all toys in the first group are harmful and all in the second group beneficial to children. I am not using the word 'amoral' to mean 'immoral'. Many of the toys that fall into this category are toys that my own children play with, and I don't think that their morals, let alone their souls, are in mortal danger as a result.

For the remainder of this chapter, I would like to discuss toys, games and other parts of the child's play world that fall into the category of the amoral.

The word in this context means that in the world in which these toys live, morals are more or less irrelevant. Evil and good are not presented as choices to be made. Good is not spelt out as being better than evil, nor is evil presented as something that is there to be defeated by good. The terms are simply not relevant.

I am deliberately using the language of the traditional fairy story rather than the language of the Bible, because fairy stories have made the terms familiar (and so have many other forms of child entertainment—such as playground games based on 'goodies' and 'baddies').

Few would quarrel with the assumption that a fairystory like *The Sleeping Beauty* takes place in a world where evil is clearly a problem; the evil witches are a threat to the good fairies. Nobody is encouraged to cheer the Witch in *The Wizard of Oz* (which is why a house can be dropped on her and few children pause to be horrified). In *Superman* comics, the hero is a transparently 'good' person, dedicated to saving the world from an obvious evil enemy. The moral framework in all these is straightforward, and one could say that all the action takes place in a fallen world, in which you can't assume that human beings will seek to do good at every opportunity, and some human beings are committed to wrongdoing: there is, in other words, something wrong with the way things are, and the job of good people is to put things right.

In the universe of the amoral toy, the Fall has never happened. The world is always bright and happy, rippled occasionally by troubles which are easily solved; every doll has a sunsuit, and every pony has big eyes and a tail you can brush.

Cuddly toys

There are a large number of toys that reflect this world. Some are cuddly dolls, others are collectables, which can be taken to bed but which reach their full play potential when surrounded by their accessories or by other similar toys.

The tradition of cuddly toys with a personality of their own is a long one, the most famous example being teddy bears. They first appeared in the opening years of the twentieth century; one legend says that the name comes from the President of the United States, Edward Roosevelt. It is claimed that the Ideal Toy Company first obtained permission to use the name, when Roosevelt was too tender-hearted to shoot a young bear cub when out bear-hunting. (An alternative claimant to the honour of inventor of the teddy bear is the German company Steiff, who are still in business today—our household possesses an endearing fluffy Steiff hedgehog.)

Today over 25% of all toys bought in the UK are teddy bears, and the value of sales in 1987 was over £40,000,000. But today there are many more cuddly toys, and also its more modern variant, the plastic collectable character doll.

Some of the latter are produced by the international giant toy companies, such as Hasbro (My Little Pony, Moon-dreamers, Sindy, Jem etc), Mattel (My Child Doll, Barbie, The Heart Family etc), Tomy (Sylvanian Families etc) and Fisher Price (Cherry, My Best Friend Dolls etc). Others are by smaller companies, and often have a much higher-quality look, such as the engaging Biggles Bear from Systema.

Many of the collectables have their own comics, such as those produced for My Little Pony, Barbie, Sylvanian Families and Care Bears; and there are many videos featuring collectable characters, usually drawn from American television shows. The comics are quite different in style, ranging from the unabashed commercialism of the My Little Pony comic to the Original Sylvanian Families comic, which has a strong emphasis on crafts and creative play.[7]

One of the most popular toys is My Little Pony.

My Little Pony

Hasbro's My Little Pony product is first and foremost a collectable, with dozens of different ponies available. The concept is brilliant: it taps the evergreen fascination of children (mainly girls, though boys seem to enjoy playing with My Little Pony as well) for horses and ponies, and combines it with the appeal of dolls that actually *do* something. My Little Ponies have manes and tails that can be brushed, and come supplied with a brush, comb or simple grooming kit; and the range includes expensive set-pieces like a grooming parlour and a riding school.

The 'adoptable' pony referred to earlier in this chapter is a good example of the My Little Pony approach. When a child joins, he or she receives the first 'Fun pack'—including the pony, an adoption certificate, an activity book and a club badge and diary. The second Fun pack is sent later: it 'will help you celebrate your Baby Pony's first birthday....' Finally:

> To make Christmas time an even happier occasion you'll really love Fun Pack three with all its festive goodies.[8]

The series concentrates on the theme common to all such toys: a sentimental, irresistible appeal. The imagery of the large dewy eyes and long, curling hair, together with the colours—either soft pastels or bright, flamboyant tones (helping to give each pony a rudimentary personality) is easily understood by a child, whose predictable response is to adore the toy in the shop and desperately wish to add it to the collection at home. Some of the ponies are bizarre—one is a unicorn—and there are some very odd accessories available, including roller skates (supplied in a set of four of course!) and a wedding kit.

Much of the My Little Pony comic is an unashamed advertisement for the range. The stories are simple in the extreme, often revolving round the arrival of new ponies in Pony Land (ie the launching of a new model in the My Little Pony range). The ponies spend their days in tranquillity, and when a problem ripples the surface, it is soon resolved.

Certainly the world of My Little Pony comic is a world largely untroubled by moral absolutes or the effects of human sinfulness. In the cartoon films, where threatening characters do appear, they are repulsed by the ponies' use of 'the power of the rainbow'. Rainbows are an element in the design of the My Little Pony logo and feature prominently in the product advertising.

Barbie and Sindy

The second example is rather different. It is much easier for a child to see correspondences between the world of Barbie and Sindy, and the real world. This is because toys like My Little Pony actually *own* very little. But Barbie and Sindy are all about possessions.

Barbie was first introduced thirty years ago. Until then, dolls had been objects to mother; playing with them, a little girl could act out a mother-role.

But Barbie was different. She was a doll to look up to, an 'aspirational toy'; blonde and beautiful, with long legs and a wasp-like waist, with glamorous clothes, wonderful make-up, and sensational hair styles.

She was dainty and feminine, but also intelligent. Every year she was given a new persona, and in her thirty years she has been an air hostess, an astronaut, a news reader, a teacher, a doctor. For many little girls, she has been the epitome of everything they would like to be. And what she offers is an expensive, fashionable look, Hollywood glamour, and clothes which are the height of expensive fashion.

Furthermore, whereas My Little Ponies live in Pony Land, Barbie and Sindy live in the 'real world'. The clothes and hair styles they wear reflect current fashion trends. The packaging reflects current leisure interests. In 1986, an actress played the part of Barbie and toured sixteen British cities with a rock group as 'Barbie and the Rock Stars.'[9]

The dolls came in a wide range. Super Hair Barbie, Tropical Barbie, Rock Star Barbie, and many more; Sindy, with her extensive range of clothes outfits; Jem, Sindy's rock star cousin (Barbie's boyfriend, Ken, also has an outfit of rock clothes and hairstyles to match). Doll houses, horses, stables, packs of shoes, and numerous other accessories are available.

Just as My Little Pony brilliantly captured the pony-mad market, so Barbie and Sindy have scooped the market occupied by any child that ever dressed a doll. By the same token, the imaginative involvement is very strong, as the child selects from the doll's wardrobe, and even goes shopping to buy outfits that will enhance the choice available.

But Barbie and Sindy are not merely to do with clothes and wardrobes. They are about lifestyle. They have lives of their own, and the clothes and accessories are designed to equip them to lead those lives. With the lifestyle comes a set of values, a statement by implication about what things are to be valued and sought after in life: fine clothes, good hair, a horse of one's own, holidays in Spain, and exotic night clubs and rock venues.

The two dolls represent competing products from two giants of the toy industry: Hasbro and Mattel. This rivalry is reflected in the fact that there is a discernible difference in the way the two dolls are presented. Sindy—though not poor, and certainly a glamorous lady—is often in the countryside, riding her horse or otherwise enjoying the fresh air. Barbie, on the other hand, is just as likely to be sipping a drink in a night club, or relaxing on the beach in the South of France.

Like My Little Pony, Barbie and Sindy live in a world comparatively untouched by moral absolutes. People in that world are happy and contented, and their life revolves around their possessions. Occasionally some problem will arise, but the danger tends to remain at the level of a possible disruption to their enjoyment.

So is there a problem?

It should be said at the outset that many toys like those we have been talking about provide good play opportunities for children, and if the value of a toy were to be measured by the amount of time a child spends playing with it, most of them would have to be considered very good buys indeed.

Their usefulness in expanding the child's imagination is, I believe, limited. Reading the My Little Pony comic aloud to a child is a very unsatisfactory experience; the child soon learns how to recognise the different ponies by name, but the language of the stories is banal and unevocative (the fact that almost every speech has an exclamation mark indicates that the authors know their text needs all the help it can get). The pictures do not have very much for the child to discover, and the links between text and pictures are shallow. By the usual criteria of excellence in children's stories, the My Little Pony comic falls down badly.

Other collectables-based comics are also of mixed value. The Care Bears comic, for example, is less of an advertisement, has some activity projects, and some good and varied artwork. But the text of the stories is uninspired, and the language level often inapproriate: in a comic selling primarily to 5–10 year olds, the snowman in the Christmas issue says things like:

> "I say, you're quick off the mark old chap! Of course I can talk. Jolly fun, what!"

which is a joke only much older children would understand (younger children laugh at the funny voice but do not know why it's funny).

Of the other two toys mentioned in this chapter, the Barbie comic really belongs with the teenage magazines discussed elsewhere in this book, and I have already mentioned the good features of the Sylvanian Families comic.

Parents will not need to be reminded of some practical problems with collectables—the sheer cost involved, and the unease that one may feel at a child investing so much of its play life in a single toy or range of toys. The whole matter of advertising of toys is a serious issue, and will be discussed in Chapter 7, but it should be pointed out that many children go through a phase of playing with such toys and eventually abandon them and go on to something else (in our family we have obtained quite a few of our own stocks from jumble sales, where other parents have dumped the relics of their own childrens' crazes).

But how much of a problem do these toys present? Is it enough to concede that they are quite weak educationally, and limited in their capacity to feed the creative imagination—but that after all other toys can be given to a child as well to remedy these defects, so that the child can have the addictive fun of the collectables and huggables, and also have his or her imagination spurred by other things?

I think that there *are* some substantial problems with toys that live in the amoral world about which we have been talking. Toys create a world, and for the period of play, a child lives in that world. It is reasonable to ask what that world is contributing to the enlarging imagination of the child.

> When we look at "My Little Pony" or at the spin-off playthings from a successful movie or television series, shouldn't we ask ourselves the question, "What does this aspect of our material culture show about our society?" "What values do the toys seek to sustain?" "What do they reveal of the world of parents and children, and of the world of work and play?"[10]

It is doubtful, too, whether a doll that defines success, personality and fun in the highly specific terms of a particular physical shape and hair colour (eg Barbie's shapely blonde) is a good role model for children who will not usually fit the pattern being prescribed for them. A model that implies that 'what you are is not enough' in this way is, ultimately, an unhealthy model.

The case of Enid Blyton

An example of the amoral world in children's books is found in parts of the work of Enid Blyton.

My view of her work is influenced by the fact that I started my working life as a librarian, and was able to observe the way that many children read her books. It was very similar to the way that many adults read popular romantic novels— they simply read the whole stock of Enid Blyton books one after the other, and when they came to the last one they started all over again.

Not all children were reading Enid Blyton like that, and some were able to dip into her work and read other authors as well. Her books, too, are not all the same. But many of her stories evoke a world which simply doesn't run in the same way as the world its readers lived in.

It's a world where children pursue foreign spies with reckless regard for their own safety, and are praised by the police (whereas any real police officer would have marched the Famous Five to their parents and demanded that they be punished for being so irresponsible, and for jeopardising the arrest of the spies!).

In that world, a youngster like Julian of the Famous Five is able to be atrociously rude to adults, and yet be praised for his wit. The Secret Seven and the Famous Five are both unkind to children outside the favoured circle, particularly if the child in question is ugly, fat, or otherwise unlike a Blyton hero or heroine. Parents and guardians revolve their lives round the children's needs.

In the world of these books, very little can be learned by the reader which will be of much use in the world outside. It would usually be disastrous to try to conduct real-life situations and relationships in the way such things are done in the books. The stories remain fantasies, contributing little, and very likely reinforcing unrealistic expectations of what life ought to be like.

Some of Enid Blyton's books are not of this type—the

school stories, for example, teach some elementary moral truths about loyalty, about how to relate to unpopular class-mates, about dignity and self-worth even if one's home back-ground is not wealthy, and so on.

But the amoral tales, with their cardboard characterisa-tion and wooden dialogue, don't teach even elementary moral truths—and they could conceivably do harm to a child.

Much the same could be said of a Barbie Doll or a My Little Pony. The child's mind is being exercised but not stretched, and its moral understanding is not being chal-lenged. There is little to involve the child. He or she is not forced to take sides on issues, and consequently to think through his or her own position on those issues. Play should be an enriching experience; it's questionable whether some of the collectables and huggables achieve much more than occupying a child's time with absorbing arrangements of colours and shapes. That in itself could be quite creative play. But the values and assumptions that are conveyed by the look and packaging of the toy are usually a high price to pay for a learning experience that other toys can give more cheaply and effectively.

Deeper issues

Some writers on toys have seen very major problems with toys like the ones we have been discussing. Phil Phillips, an American writer, has argued that occult and New Age influ-ences abound in My Little Pony, Care Bears, Smurfs, Cab-bage Patch Kids, and several other mass-market toys.

Phillips's book[11] is distributed in Britain, and his concern for children is shared by many people. I do not think that he has proved his point, and we will be returning to his thesis later in this book. But I am entirely in sympathy with his basic position: that we cannot treat our children's toys as 'mere playthings'. We must see them as influences that are helping to shape and mould our children's minds, whether the toy be a fantasy monster or a lovable pony with hair that you can brush.

In this chapter we have looked at a number of products that might not seem at first to have anything to say to children at all, and have considered a few of the ways in which messages, values and attitudes do come across to children.

In the next chapter we will be looking at a whole category of toy in which the messages are often very explicit, and the context of a struggle between good and evil is actually woven into the product and its packaging. It sounds great news for Christians. But there are problems.

4

The World of Right and Wrong

He [Stan Lee, the creative mind behind many comic book heroes] sees the superhero fantasies as fulfilling the same function that myths, legends, tales of romance and fairy stories did for earlier generations.

The Penguin Book of Comics[1]

Not all the collectable toys on toyshop shelves are like the ones we have been looking at in the last chapter. Some are posed in fighting attitudes; others wear costumes identifying them as evil villains or pure, selfless heroes; most have accessories, and almost all have some sort of book, video or comic backup. When we watch the video, look at the comic or read the book, we find that the toy is a combatant in a cosmic battle.

The heroic figure stands confidently, his mighty limbs poised for action, his great sword unsheathed. He is young, blonde, handsome, and strong.

I am Adam: Prince of Eternia and defender of the secrets of Castle Grayskull.... Fabulous secret powers were revealed to me the day I held aloft my magic sword and said, "By the power of Grayskull—*I have the power!*"

His voice reverberates through space as he continues:

...and I became He-Man—the most powerful man in the universe!

And as the opening credits come to an end, we are launched into another episode of *He-Man and the Masters of the Universe*, in which He-Man will be locked in mortal struggle with Skeletor or Hordak, his evil opponents.

In the *Masters of the Universe* toys, magazines, television shows and videos, we are clearly in a very different world from that which we saw in the last chapter. It is a world where evil and good are defined sharply and given bodily form. It is a world that is under threat from evil, where the hero is a champion of good, and those who serve evil are clearly shown as being morally wrong, whereas those who help or serve He-man are shown to be morally right. Something is wrong with this world, and whatever it is that is wrong is a corrupting force that can make people slaves to evil against their will. And that evil is masterminded by an evil intelligence that walks the world of Eternia.

London Magazines, who publish the *Masters of the Universe Adventure Magazine*, have provided a history of Eternia and the origins of He-Man in a free mini-comic, *The Origin of He-Man*.[2] In it we read of the early days of Eternia, 'once ruled by a noble and peaceful royal family, who enforced honesty and justice for all'. Castle Grayskull was created by a Council of Elders to protect Eternia from the evil that they saw would one day come. The Castle waited through the ages until Prince Adam was born and came to manhood, and the sorceress who was the guardian of the castle knew that he was the mortal destined to protect Eternia against Skeletor, Hordak and all evil.

Skeletor was the essence of evil, intent on conquering Eternia as a springboard to domination of the universe. He had betrayed his tutor, Hordak, who is now pursuing him for vengeance and has also set his sights on capturing Eternia as the first step in universal domination.

To help him in his fight, Adam is given the Sword of Power, the knowledge of the secrets of Grayskull, and the ability to transform himself at will into He-Man, in the way described above. He gathers round him a band of the mightiest champions on Eternia, and, as the Masters of the Universe, they make their base in the Royal Palace of Eternos City. From there they set out on adventures to defend Castle Grayskull, which holds the secrets of the universe, or to prevent Eternia being subjugated by the forces of Skeletor and Hordak.

Those readers who are Christians (or who follow another faith) will recognise the strong religious motifs in this comic and running through the He-Man stories. They include: the existence of a personal devil; the powerlessness of humanity to resist that devil by their own strength; the need for a saviour who will take up the task of defeating the evil one; and the distinction between mercy and merit—salvation in *He-Man* doesn't only come to those who have deserved it, but also to those who need it and have no way of their own of achieving it.

There are major differences too, of course; for example, only a few people know about Prince Adam's superpersonality and supernatural powers. In order to avoid his other persona becoming widely known, he affects a timid and lazy manner. Most religions teach that the claims of their saviour or prophet were made openly, and were widely known.

But the religious overtones lend depth and colour to the theme of good and evil which is developed in *Masters of the Universe*, and in the many similar products that work the same way.

For there are many toys of this type. To begin with there is Adam's twin sister Adora, who metamorphoses into She-ra, Princess of Power. Others that are perpetually engaged in a struggle between good and evil are Tonka's 'Supernaturals' and the prolific Superman industry, which has a number of spin-offs.

Cinema, television and toys

Many contemporary films explore the same theme of the struggle between good and evil. One example is George Lucas's *Star Wars* trilogy, which has been phenomenally successful. Its appeal to children is simple and direct.

> He intended his film, Lucas confesses, for a generation growing up without fairy tales. His target audience was fourteen years and younger.... It was a celebration, a social affair, a collective drama, and people came again and again, dragging their friends and families with them.[3]

The *Star Wars* series explores the theme of a dark empire threatening to enslave the universe. It features a rallying-cry for the good—'May the Force be with you'—and a wide range of robots and aliens, most of which have endeared themselves to child audiences: characters such as C-3PO (affectionately called Threepio) and R2-D2 the bickering robots, Obi-Wan Kenobi the guide and counsellor, Yoda the sage, and the cuddly Ewoks. The two protagonists, Darth Vader and Luke Skywalker, have become as well known in popular child literature as Robin Hood was in earlier times.

Robin Hood himself has recently made a come-back on television with an updated version starring Jason Connery. The stories have the same emphasis on helping the poor at the expense of the rich, but Robin is given an almost religious significance and distinct supernatural and occult overtones by the inclusion in the plot of his sorcerer adviser.

The good/evil battle is the thrust of most children's television fiction, and the programmes link in with current toy and game interests. An example is *Nightmare*, a programme based on fantasy role-playing games such as *Dungeons and Dragons*. In this television game, teams of children guide one of their members blindfold through a beautifully-crafted fantasy environment (a dungeon, castle, etc) under the supervision of a spectacular referee figure who corresponds to the Dungeon Master in more conventional fantasy role-

playing games.[4] The nominated child tries to survive monsters, traps and various other hazards, and his team-mates
direct him with advice and messages.

Fantasy games

Nightmare has also appeared as a traditional board game,
but its origins are clearly in the fantasy role-playing (FRP)
games that are currently enormously popular. An indication
of their popularity is the number of magazines on sale in
High Street newsagents. Titles like *White Dwarf* contain
articles and advice on how to take part in, or run, fantasy
games, and they provide background material and other help
for people designing their own fantasy game-worlds.

I have dealt with this subject at length in *Children at Risk*.
But it is relevant to say here that the fantasy game industry is
changing. An increasing number of games are set in fantasy
worlds other than the traditional FRP dungeons or other
medieval environments. New ways of playing, such as Play-
by-Mail, computer FRP, and telephone games such as Computerdial's FIST (Fantasy Interactive Scenarios by Telephone) are popular. Telephone computer games are played
by several people simultaneously, each player's computer
being linked to the game administrator's computer by a
telephone link.

> FIST is a stunningly realistic adventure challenge crafted by
> genius game-master Steve Jackson and the computer wizardry
> of Computerdial Limited.
>
> Discover an entirely new concept of fantasy gaming, an awe-
> somely different world that awaits beyond your telephone. Dial
> Fist and you unlock a living, breathing, terror-stalked world of
> mediaeval fantasy.
>
> You are a warrior within this thrillingly realistic adventure,
> that you control every step of the way simply by using the
> numbers on your telephone; while a trusted guide offers action,
> advice and the corresponding numbers that determine your
> moves.[5]

Fantasy worlds

Fantasy role-playing games are the most complete way that an act of play takes the player into a new world of the imagination. Anybody wanting to gain an overview of the present state of the FRP hobby would find it useful to look at a magazine such as *G.M.: the Independent Fantasy Roleplaying Magazine*. The January 1989 issue contains an interview with Gary Gygax, who was the main figure behind the creation of *Dungeons and Dragons*. Gygax said:

> In my youth, I found fairy tales, legends, myths, and all fantasy absolute captivation. I can recall my very early years, the time when age is reckoned in months, not years. From *The Tale of the Three Billy Goats Gruff* to the wonderful bedtime stories my father created for my amusement, I loved the realms of fantastic imaginings.[6]

FRP also has a well-defined basic structure of good versus evil. I have discussed the limitations and problems of this in the context of FRP elsewhere,[7] but almost all games of this type at least concede the fact that the world does operate within a moral framework.

This is, for example, characteristic of the world of *2000 AD*, a popular comic selling to chidren and adults, on which the FRP game *Judge Dredd* is based. Set in a vastly expanded New York in the year 2000 AD, it presents a picture of a multi-level metropolis in which lawlessness is rife. In pursuit of the lawbreakers come the lawmen, the Judges, who ride mighty motor-cycles and wear fearsome armour.

The abiding principle of the world of *2000 AD* is 'The Law'.

> A Judge cannot and must not simply go around shooting anyone he feels like whenever it takes his fancy! That would be a breach of The Law, and a Judge who breaks the Law is not worthy of his badge, or of anything else either; the penalty for any Judge who breaks the Law is a minimum of 20 years of hard labour on

the prison planet Titan. A Judge's job is to take people alive, so that they can serve their time in prison. *Judges are not executioners*.[8]

Judge Dredd is one of the most popular FRP games in Britain today, partly because it is humorous, partly because it plays well, partly because players enjoy the unusual setting: but also, I am sure, due in a great part to the fact that it presents a vivid imaginative world, running on recognisably moral lines, in which players can join forces in the face of evil. In this respect, it is in the same category as *Star Wars* and many other contemporary classics.

Conclusion

This chapter began with a description of a game that features a champion of the weak and oppressed, looking beyond human limitations towards a supernatural source of power with which to do good.

It ends with a description of a game in which players act out the roles of Judges seeking out law-breakers and bringing them to justice.

Many Christian parents are frustrated by the saccharine world of My Little Pony and fashionable dolls, and wish that there were toys and games that had more content. The toys that have been described in this chapter certainly fit that description.

Sounds good?

To a certain extent it certainly does, and I would suggest that there is a good deal for parents to appreciate in these toys, and that valuable lessons are conveyed through the immense playability and addictiveness of many of these products.

But I would suggest that we need more. If children *are* influenced by play, and if the imaginative world into which play leads them is as absorbing as I have suggested, then toys and games should be as rich and fulfilling as possible, not just on the level of playability and durability, but also on the level of how the toy relates to the world in which the child will one day have to make its own way.

Seen from that perspective, the majority of toys and games, I would argue, fall short. Indeed, they only go half way.

5

Half-way Heroes

If you can dream it, you can *be* it. That's what role-playing is all about.... After all, playing the games...and dreaming the dreams...is what it's all about.

Avalon Hill Advertisement[1]

The emphasis on good versus evil that is found in many toys and comics today, featuring a champion of good—usually equipped with superhuman powers and a strong commitment to law and order—goes back to the beginning of storytelling. Odysseus wandering the world fighting monsters, Arthur's knights riding in pursuit of noble causes to champion, the heroes of the Icelandic sagas—these and many more played out their quests against the backdrop of a world where the stark alternatives of right and wrong were more clear-cut than they are today.

That's probably a part of the appeal that moral quests have for us; they make easily-understandable choices in settings far removed from the complexity of modern life. It would be easy to do the right thing, we feel, if matters were as simple as they seem to be in *Superman* and *Masters of the Universe*.

To that extent toys, comics, films and videos featuring such themes can be welcomed by Christian parents as a step in the right direction. There is a real sense in which children are receiving a much clearer message about morality from a

She-ra or *Spiderman* film than they will ever get from *Dallas* or *Dynasty*, where the 'goodies' are never quite so watchable as the 'baddies' (where would *Dallas* be without J. R.?). It is worthwhile to reaffirm, as many comics do, that morality is in essence a system of choices, and that the basic choices are in reality very simple.

But it is also true that the bald simplicity of the average comic tends to produce a very one-dimensional morality, so there are no wider implications to distract from the power of the message. It's simply the satisfaction of a job well done; Skeletor is vanquished, Batman defeats the Joker, Wonder Woman sees justice done. They always end up victorious and in control, because that is what they are there for. They are the superheroes, the saviours of mankind, who come to rescue people from that from which they cannot save themselves.

Saviour credentials

It is at this point that alarm bells should begin to ring for Christian parents. It is one thing to be cast in the role of a saviour of the oppressed and champion of good against evil. He-Man, for example, operating in a cosmos dominated by the struggle between himself and his fellow-heroes, and the evil Skeletor and Hordak and their allies, represents an acceptable statement of the eternal conflict between good and evil, and man's need for a power greater than himself.

But it's a different matter when *a* saviour becomes *the* saviour, when the comic-book, character-doll heroes are the only saviours there are. Characters such as He-Man and the Masters of the Universe are presented as the saviours of mankind (in that the inhabitants of Eternia seem not very different from ourselves), and Christian parents, who find in the Bible a very complete description of what to look for in a saviour, may well want to look closely at the model which is being presented to children in this way. And when we do look closely, we find some problems.

To place the discussion in context, it's necessary to look at a little history.

The Comics Code

The link between comics and toys in the area we are talking about in this chapter is very strong. But seeing problems in comics is not a new phenomenon. Concern over comics goes back many years.

Although comic strips have existed for much longer, comics as we know them today began in the 1930s and 1940s, when Superman, Batman, Captain America, the Human Torch, Wonder Woman and others who are still published today became enormously popular. During the Second World War sales reached 15,000,000 a month, the total readership was 50,000,000, and American servicemen away from home read the comics avidly and nostalgically.

In the war years, too, images of strong deliverers rescuing oppressed and vulnerable people had an obvious relevance. That was what both American and British understood the fighting to be about, and the comics backed up the mission of deliverance with a ready-made mythology. So the super-heroes of the comics, fighting Lex Luthor and a gallery of other villains, chimed with the West's preoccupation with the much more serious and deadly struggle going on in the theatres of war.

After the war, the comics remained popular. The big publishers continued with the series that had already proved their popularity, and smaller publishers, seeing the potential, produced smaller and often shoddier comics.

But an increasing number of people began to suggest that the new comic industry had problems.

For one thing, the scale of the struggles portrayed had enlarged: the world had passed through a major catastrophic war which had left few communities untouched, and people understood what tragedy was. After all, many had only recently fought in the hell of the trenches, or had lived as civilians in cities that had died in flames. They understood that you need a super-hero to deal with a super-evil.

But as the heroes grew more powerful, the villains became more evil. There grew up a publishing industry, around the major publishers, which exploited the new context of fear, and produced pulp horror that was unlike anything that had appeared on news-stands previously. Though the major publishers were not part of the opportunist substructure, the pulp market had an inevitable effect on the mainstream comics, whose heroes became more wondrous and whose villains more villainous.

Protests against the new 'horror comics' were made by worried parents, educationalists, and others. But it was the work of Frederic Wertham, a hospital psychiatrist, that triggered a campaign with the publication in 1954 of his book *Seduction of the Innocent*. It is helpful to consider the campaign briefly, because the issues are still very relevant today.

The horror comics campaign

Wertham set out to examine the relationship between juvenile mental and behavioural problems, and comics. His work has been criticised in many quarters. One of his strongest critics in Britain is Martin Barker, who has researched the British horror comics campaign of the 1950s. His book on the subject is well-researched and thoughtful.[2] He makes the points that have been made by other commentators: that Wertham's case only had real validity against the fringe publishers; that his criticisms against the major publishers tended to ignore evidence that they themselves were aware of problems and that their portrayal of violence was of a very different order from that of the pulp comics; and that Wertham had failed completely to understand the sociological significance of the comics, what they were trying to achieve, the context of the violence and horror they portrayed, and the ominous political overtones of suppression and censorship.

Some of these arguments are good ones. Christian critics of the media today, for example, often fall into the trap, as Wertham himself did, of not distinguishing between two quite different things.

There is enormous difference, for example, between the violence of a film like *Bad Timing* (shown recently on television in Britain, though in the late evening) and the violence in a cartoon film like *Tom and Jerry*. And the violence of *The A-Team* is a different kind of violence again, and so is that of a film like *Rocky*.[3] When we say 'There is too much violence on TV', we *must* tackle the question of 'What sorts of violence?'.

Wertham also often failed to put horror into its context. From the comics he collected examples of severed heads, human remains, violent shootings, and other horrors. Today Christians have often collected incidences of swearing on television. But in both cases, the context can make a difference. The Bible itself contains passages that are gruesome but nevertheless fair descriptions in context.

There was a massive outcry when a private blasphemy, uttered under great stress and, it later turned out, physical pain (though no less a blasphemy because of that) was accidentally broadcast by Richard Dimbleby. But there is a world of difference between that and the casual, non-stop swearing of a TV stand-up comic, or the indiscriminate use of sexual swearing in a light comedy. But many Christian commentators today do not make that distinction, and their researches are only of limited value.

For example, we cannot measure change if we don't analyse. If in one year 90 per cent of the swearing on TV was in soap opera and 10 per cent in serious drama, and in the following year only 40 per cent was in soap opera and 60 per cent in serious drama, then whatever one's overall view, it would have to be conceded that there had been a massive reduction in popular media swearing, even though there were still exactly the same number of swear words on TV— an extreme example, admittedly, but it makes the point.

One more criticism of Wertham's work which I think has some validity is that he sometimes didn't give credit for existing anxieties on the part of publishers. Many mainline comic publishers were already concerned, and their products were different from those of their pulp rivals. And today, credit is often not given for forces in the media, entertainment and leisure industries who are trying to change things. It's all too easy to see an industry as monolithic, all of the same kind, all to be reacted to and dealt with in the same way.

Wertham's contribution

Why then did I put Frederic Wertham's name as one of the dedicatees of *Children at Risk* (and thereby invite—and receive—some quite negative comments!)? The reason is that I believe Wertham served children well in the work he did, and that parents should be grateful to him.

Firstly, he realised that whatever the rationale for comics, and whatever social or recreational value they may have had, the fact that they were freely available to small children was something that needed to be stopped. Today, when similar defences of 'video nasties' and other publications are being made—that they fulfil a valuable function, that they are social documents, that they are a critique of society—it is important that people should responsibly weigh the potential value against the potential harm. The case against video nasties in Graham Bright's campaign (which culminated in the 1984 Video Recordings Act) was not primarily a critique of the videos as art objects, but a determination to keep them out of the hands of children. The initial contact with

Graham Bright at the very beginning of the parliamentary campaign was a teachers' lobby.[4]

Secondly, he showed individual parents, teachers and citizens that their voice counted. His campaign was a grassroots campaign, waged by customers in supermarkets, teachers in schools, individuals in their ordinary everyday environments. By mobilising shoppers to boycott shops that sold comics which they objected to, he succeeded in forcing the publishers to listen to the voice of the community.

I do not think that one has to agree with Frederic Wertham's analysis in total before one can admire what he achieved. Today, many who would be cautious about fully subscribing to the aims and agenda of Mary Whitehouse's National Viewers' and Listeners' Association are nevertheless appreciative of her work in demonstrating that you don't have to be a trained orator or an expert media person before you can register concern with broadcasters.

Wertham's legacy

The American campaign was followed closely by a British campaign, largely aimed at imported American horror comics. But the supply of these did not survive for long. In America, the comic industry was taking a new direction.

In an attempt to avoid government-imposed controls following Wertham's campaign, the industry set up a self-regulating organisation, the Comics Code Authority. Like Advertising Standards Authority and the Press Council in Britain, the Authority was a voluntary institution, to impose standards.

All the major comic publishers were involved, with the exception of the Dell Publishing company, who considered that their publications were of a high standard already. The fringe publishers—who had been responsible for the material which had caused Wertham greatest concern—faded from the comics scene.

Today, there is a strong adult comics readership, and new developments include the graphic novel, a comic treatment in book-length form. Britain, Japan, and other countries are experiencing a comics revival.

The comics boom can cause some problems; for example, the satirical *Oink!* and the gruesome and visually disturbing *Bad Company* (QC Comics) are both often to be found in newsagents stacked with comics intended for a much younger readership.

Published more with children in mind are several toy-related comics from Marvel Comics and DC Comics. And, though many of today's comics for older readers are strident, lurid, and violent (and often thereby have something valid to say about the kind of world we live in), the industry still evidently exercises a measure of self-restraint and applies self-imposed standards.

A moral code

When we look at an American comic today, therefore, we are looking at something which comes from a tradition of moral entertainment and responsibility towards young readers.

The morality of comics is strong. The villains who are vanquished are all people who ought to be vanquished, the motives of the heroes are good motives, and they persevere in their efforts to save human beings even though they are usually fighting the forces of evil at every step. These heroes *care*—otherwise they would go off and live an easier life.

The problems, I believe, are all in the fact that comic-book morality doesn't go far enough.

Half-way morality

One very limited moral fable is that found in some collectable toys, where a rudimentary championing of right takes place, but the story-world is so cosy and hard to take seriously that it's hard to accept the story as a moral code.

An example is Care Bears and their associated films, magazines and accessories.

Care Bears

Care Bears are manufactured by an American company called Those Characters From Cleveland Inc. The toy bears are backed up by a range of accessories, including videos, and a comic which is published by Marvel Comics.

The nineteen Care Bears live in Care-a-Lot, a land above the clouds, where they eat off cloud-tables and sleep on cloud-beds. When they are needed in the world below, the Care Alarm sounds, and they set off to help.

The Bears are summoned in situations of need, but they usually have difficulty finding where the need is, and they often make mistakes. In 'The Poor Little Rich Girl', a story in the Care Bears comic,[5] they are summoned to help a little girl who lives in a rich mansion. Her name is Missy Moneyworth, and she is crying because her 'very expensive skateboard' is broken.

Funshine Bear, Wish Bear and Bedtime Bear go down (via a rainbow) to her family mansion, leaving Grams Bear and the others behind. However, as they get there her parents arrive ('They drove here from a far away wing of the mansion') with a fabulously expensive replacement; a robot rock group. 'Oh, thank you, Mums and Dads! It's the best toy I ever had!' screams the little girl. Returning to Care-a-Lot, Funshine Bear calls out cheerily to Grams, 'We weren't needed down below after all!'

'Then why is the Care Alarm still ringing so loudly?' asks Grams, and the episode (to be continued next week) ends with the Bears' dawning realisation of what the reader has been given heavy hints towards all through the story: expensive toys aren't going to make this little girl happy.

The bears make a similar mistake in the Care Bears video 'The Long Lost Care Bears',[6] where they answer a Care Alarm from a distant idyllic valley. Their rescue of the two bears who live there, and their attempts to teach them how to become Care Bears, turn out to be well-meant but misguided, when it is revealed that the presence of the two bears (who turn out to be long-lost relatives of the Care Bears) is in fact the reason that the valley stays perpetually springlike and beautiful; their absence in Care-a-Lot has doomed the valley to a perpetual frozen winter. The video ends with the two valley bears managing to put matters right, though the Care Bears do help them enthusiastically.

Care Bears are less a team of good and benevolent immortals coming to aid a weak humanity, than a family of rather foolish but well-meaning—and extremely huggable—toys that blunder through to some sort of realisation that most problems in life can be dealt with by caring and loving. Their ultimate weapon in the cause of Caring is the Care Stare, a force-beam that is projected from the symbols they wear on their tummies. But it is a curiously all-purpose weapon, as useful for creating a snow-cloud as for defeating an evil monster.[7]

He-Man and She-ra

A more defined morality is to be found in the He-Man and She-ra toys, films and publications. Yet when one looks closely, it is apparent that He-Man's 'saviour-hood' is also an incomplete one. What earns him the right to save the world? Not a superhuman moral purity. He isn't a holier person, or a better person, or a more spiritual person, than the inhabitants of Eternia. Neither is it a Creator's power over his creation. He-Man is simply stronger than they are, and he wields a sword that gives him miraculous powers.

The link between humanity and its rescuer—Adam becomes He-Man, Clark Kent becomes Superman, and so on—and the fact that most of the human identities of the superheroes are humdrum and unimpressive, is an echo of the incarnation; Jesus became man.

Christian symbolism permeates the comics. But the essence of the Christian gospel is that Jesus was able to be the saviour of the world not because he was stronger, but because he was *better* than us. He was born in weakness and public disgrace, and grew up as an artisan in an occupied country. But he never committed a single wrongdoing, and that was the sole mark of his saviourhood. He was perfect.

In the comics, however, goodness, purity, holiness and such concepts are used very little. He-Man is *strong*, and he has access to supernatural powers.

> In his other guise of the weakling Prince Adam, He-Man was at the Palace of Eternia, talking to his mother, the Queen. When Teela's cry for help reached him, he left the palace and raised his sword. "By the power of Grayskull!" he cried—and became He-Man.[8]

She-ra, his sister, can also summon up supernatural powers:

> Princess Adora did what she could to help but as things grew worse, she made up her mind. This was a task for She-ra, Princess of Power. In a secret glade she drew her sword and cried,
> "FOR THE HONOUR OF GRAYSKULL!"
> Instantly she was She-ra, Princess of Power.[9]

In their heroic personas they are physically magnificent: She-ra is beautiful, He-man superbly muscled.

Right through might

This morality of strength is not diametrically opposed to the biblical concept of saviourhood. It merely leaves the most important parts out. Nevertheless, much of the story has biblical echoes. He-Man's task is often threatened by a temporary victory of the evil powers, from which he is freed by a weaker character, often a child; so his great strength is not infallible. Also teamwork is emphasised, and the biblical values of kindness and compassion are usually affirmed.

I don't think that a child's soul is in danger if he or she plays with He-Man and She-ra toys. The fantasies they enact with them will at least contain a positive good-versus-evil confrontation. The problem is that children who are being taught about Jesus at Sunday School, and play with such toys in the week, have two competing models of saviourhood presented to them. Which will attract their imagination more strongly? Adults who are responsible for teaching young people about Christianity need to look at toys like He-Man, and at the TV programmes, comics, books and cassettes that accompany them.

You are not teaching Christianity in a vacuum. You are, as it were, offering goods in a market where there are competing stalls. The full-blooded gospel is more dynamic and exciting than any children's story; but it is possible to make it dreary and uninteresting.

Those who are not Christians ought to look closely at these toys too, I believe. A morality of strength is a difficult position to maintain in the modern world, where the good are often weak, and the evil are often the ones who have the almost supernatural power. Children need to be taught at an early age that doing good and choosing the right thing rather than the wrong will often bring ridicule and unpopularity, and such situations will not always—or even often—end up in scenes of triumphant vindication such as happens at the end of a He-Man video.

Should toys like this be banned? Definitely not. Children need fantasy, and He-Man has a good deal in common with traditional fables of childhood. But their messages need to be balanced by other teaching, whether that teaching is given in play, by books, by formal teaching or by giving them other toys as well.

The marketing of Superman

Half-way morality can lead to problems of consistency, and nowhere more so than in the development of the Superman story in comics and films.

Superman was one of the earliest comic-book heroes. He was born on the planet Krypton, and sent to earth by his parents when his own planet was about to blow up. It's significant that his creator, Jerry Siegel, described him as:

> A character like Samson, Hercules and all the strong men I ever heard tell of rolled into one.[10]

Growing up on earth as mild-mannered Clark Kent, he roamed the world rescuing the victims of accident, crime and oppression, bringing villains to justice and averting catastrophes by using his super-speed, x-ray vision, or other facilities. There was only one thing that could harm the 'Man of Steel': Kryptonite, a substance created from the explosion of the planet Krypton, and capable of sapping Superman's mighty powers.

As a comic-book hero, Superman was extremely moral. In conformity to the Comics Code, sex didn't appear in Superman comics, and Lois Lane, who adored him, never knew that in everyday life Superman was actually the short-sighted, dull colleague who worked with her on the *Daily Planet* newspaper.

The Superman films, however, changed all that. In Superman I, when Superman is sent to earth, his father sends with him a hologram of himself, uttering words of counsel and wisdom. As a youth, Superman builds an ice palace at the Pole and enshrines the hologram there, and goes to the place regularly to listen to his father's wisdom. Among the teaching that he receives is a solemn commandment never to tamper with the natural, physical laws of the planet whose people he has come to protect.

But at the end of the film Lois Lane is trapped underground by an earthquake, and Superman—already much

more interested in her than he was when in the comic—
desperately looks for a solution. He hits on the idea of flying
very quickly round and round the earth, making the planet
rotate backwards and time itself run backwards. When he
returns to earth, it is five minutes before the earthquake and
Lois is safe.

But to be a saviour—to carry out his redemptive task—
he has had to reject a fundamental part of his 'theology', the
system of teaching which his father has taught him in the ice
palace over the years.

Matters become worse in the second Superman film,
where Lois discovers that Clark Kent *is* Superman (much to
the distress of thousands of loyal readers of the comic), and
he makes love to her. Moreover he sleeps with her in the ice
palace itself, the very place where his earthly mission has
been defined.

To be moral, to be a saviour, he has to contradict the
whole nature of his saviourhood. It is a far cry at this point
from the comics, which often speak of resolute, unflinching
consistency of purpose:

> Fear is not a conquering thing to him; he knows the power of
> fear is a lie; he knows that fear can triumph only when the will is
> weak; and he has strength of will in almost infinite amount....
> Yes, he feels the icy touch of fear, but he is not cowed. He is
> Superman.[11]

Do the young people who watch the films, read the
comics, and play with the toys based on them, identify the
conflict? I doubt it very much. But I suspect that they realise
something is not quite right, and my own conversations with
children have tended to bear this out.

The machine as hero

I have often wondered whether it is an unexpressed dissatis-
faction with human—and superhuman—saviours that has
led to the popularity of machines as heroic champions. For

example Transformers, a line of toys and comics that feature machines with personalities:

> Wreck-Gar and Rodimus Prime: they're real heroes.... Rodimus Prime: The autobot protector with the mobile defence bay. He's a hot headed hero. Wreck-Gar: He's a futuristic motorbike and the wacky leader of the junkions. Watch out for Wreck-Gar.... If you're an autobot and you're in trouble, send for Wreck-Gar and Rodimus Prime. They're real heroes! And they're in the shops now![12]

Transformers are weird constructions which break down into whole armies of weapons and vehicles. They are cleverly designed, of great manipulative appeal to the child, and very collectable.

A similar toy is Zoids, among others. They fight out the age-old war of good versus evil, clashing on strange alien plains on distant planets. Whatever they are, they are not human beings. Perhaps the children who play with them recognise that these heroes are unlikely to have the inconsistencies of a Superman. You won't find a Transformer having an affair with Lois Lane.

Judge Dredd

Perhaps that accounts, too, for the popularity of Judge Dredd and the comic *2000 AD*, which we looked at in the previous chapter. The comic has a circulation of 113,000 and the game drawn from it is one of the best-selling fantasy role-playing games in Britain.

2000 AD is a British comic, and the game is a British game. It is however set in America, in an urban megapolis of the future, where crime is widespread and lawlessness prevails. In this bleak, vast city, the Judges seek out law-breakers and do justice.

> One time, a hip Juve could only sit and *read* of Mega-City One in the pages of *2000 AD* comic, and merely *dream* of stalking its deadly streets at the side of that most famous of lawmen, Judge

Dredd. With *Judge Dredd—the Role-Playing Game*, however, you can really be there, patrolling the Meg-Ways and Under-zooms on your Lawmaster bike, on the lookout for dangerous Perps to arrest.[13]

It is a sombre vision of a future urban environment not far removed from films such as Stanley Kubrick's *A Clockwork Orange* or Derek Jarman's *Jubilee*; both pictures of the not-too distant future, where society has become vulnerable to the collapse of law—as if the film-makers were gripped by a weird nostalgia for their own future.

It may be that the Judges, who wear armoured uniform, ride armoured bikes and wear helmets and masks, are themselves the ideal combination for a fantasy hero; human inside the uniform, prone to be fallible and therefore needing the two thick volumes of rules and guidance contained in the role-playing game. But once the uniform is on, they might as well be machines—their humanity shrouded in metallic wraps, their faces masked, their pursuit of evildoers made mighty by the Lawmaster bike.

May the Force be with you...

Toys, I have been arguing, are influencing our children in many ways. They communicate values, such as Barbie Doll's luxurious lifestyle and perfect figure; and sometimes they communicate messages, such as the message of the Care Bears, that there isn't much in life that can't be sorted out with a good deal of caring and a lot of hugs.

What then are the messages coming from the toys and comics we have been considering in this chapter?

They are varied, and it is difficult to categorise them in terms of 'harmful' and 'non-harmful'. But some key messages are obvious enough. Here are three.

The human race needs someone/something bigger/stronger than itself to deal with its problems. Christian parents will not have much to argue with in that proposition. But is it adequate to leave it there? How much more can a child understand? How much more does a child need to know? Quite a bit, I would suggest.

If you summon supernatural help your problem will always be solved. But what about the times when it doesn't work like that? When the beloved pet dies after all? When the school bully doesn't leave you alone? For Christian parents, this is a problem. Unless children are taught carefully about prayer, God is going to seem very mean or at best ineffectual when compared with what Superman, He-Man and others achieve when called upon.

The force of Good is a mysterious, impersonal power. Thus the power of Grayskull, and the Force in *Star Wars*. Christian parents will recognise that this power compares badly with the Holy Spirit, who is personal and who also empowers men and women to work miracles. But it is a rare child who finds teaching about the Holy Spirit as exciting as a He-Man cartoon, and it is a crucial and challenging task for adults to make it so.

Conclusion

The toys and comics we have been talking about in this chapter are problematic, but they are not, I would suggest, a campaigning issue.

They present a moral structure and a world that runs by conventional definitions of right and wrong, and for that we must be grateful. I would rather my children played at being He-Man or She-ra than that they played at being characters from television's *Eastenders*. Though many of the comics are read by adults as much as by children, the moral choices portrayed in them are easily understood by children, and they can identify a wrong choice and trace its consequences in the plot.

However, they portray a morality that is incomplete and based almost entirely on strength. (Where a supernatural force is involved, such as the 'power of the sky' which occasionally helps He-Man, that too can only be harnessed by somebody with the mental and physical strength to do so.) For Christian parents, as we have suggested, that should be a cause for concern. But for any parent, the implications are troubling.

If a child is receiving daily the impression that morality is to be enforced through strength, will it affect his adult perceptions? Politically there is good reason to be disturbed if nations believe that the only way to bring about morality or justice is by force. The arrogance of power is a dangerous thing. A diet of Superman, He-Man and other super-heroes at least opens the mind to the possibility that that is the proper way to organise a moral crusade.

How can we handle comics and hero-toys?

We can identify the good and helpful images in them and make sure that the child has recognised them as central in the play world of the toy. Eternia is a place where certain lessons are learned, and those lessons are sometimes useful ones for real life.

We can also identify the unhelpful elements, and make a point of bringing the conversation round to such matters when talking with the child. As with television, an influence discussed is a less powerful influence, because it is then filtered through a logical thought-process.

This doesn't mean dominating the child, or cross-examining him or her at every opportunity. It means seizing opportunities when they arise, to discuss questions when events suggest them. It means being available, being the kind of parent who is there to be talked to, rather than being remote and aloof. It means taking play seriously, and recognising that a child at play is often thinking very deeply.

It means, in fact, sharing the play-life of your child; not as a spy or a censor, but as a sounding-board, somebody who has taken time to look at the toys and other play resources and has taken them at more than face value.

It may seem like hard work, it may seem like idealism. But it pays great dividends, and is worth making space for in our busy lives. Play is an important part of our children's lives, and building communication between parents and children involves developing some understanding of the things that are important to them.

Many aspects of children's play are of little practical interest to adults. There's not much to be learned from helping to brush a toy pony's tail, arranging a council of the Masters of the Universe, or choosing an outfit for Sindy to wear to her next party. But time spent sharing these activities is a time of closeness; one of your few opportunities to meet with your child on ground that is important to the child rather than you.

And that is when the best conversations about toys take place—as you hold the toys in your hands. Children lead too active and busy lives to be able to postpone the debate until a more suitable time.

6

Playing with Problems

Pandora has been elected Form Captain. We had a secret ballot. There are 29 in our form. She got 28 votes and I got one. I voted for myself. I hope she doesn't find out.

Pandora asked me not to stand outside her house and stare up at her window after dark. She said it gave her the creeps.

The Adrian Mole Diary 1986[1]

Sue Townsend's brilliant creation, Adrian Mole (aged 13¾), rapidly became a household name.

Adrian's world, revolving round a fourteen-year-old feminist, an eighty-nine-year-old chain smoker, a spoiled best friend and various tensions between his parents, is a world of constant worry. He worries about his family, he worries about his relationship with Pandora, he worries about his physical development, and he worries about getting spots.

Sue Townsend's achievement was to capture the strange dislocation of the early teenage years; a time when children are either pre-pubescent, going through puberty, or having recently passed puberty; and the changes in their bodies are matched only by the unsettling changes in the way they think about their immediate environment.

Adolescents...experience their daydreams as something gloomy and one might say almost tiring. When one has worked a great deal with adolescents, one becomes very aware of the distinction they draw between their daydreams and their 'dreams', in the sense of projects. Having dreams in that sense is something that moves forward, whereas daydreaming is something closed, something that catches you in its toils, something that swirls about you like fog. It's like a grey, drizzly day.[2]

Author and advertising executive Malcolm Doney has neatly described adolescence as a time when 'problems and acne come to a head'.[3] James Dobson, writing on the subject of children and discipline, has this to say about adolescence:

The period of early adolescence is typically a painful time of life, marked by rapid physical and emotional changes.... The thirteenth and fourteenth years commonly are the most difficult twenty-four months in life. It is during this time that self-doubt and feelings of inferiority reach an all-time high, amidst the greatest social pressures yet experienced.[4]

Benjamin Spock, whose *Baby and Child Care* has sold well over 20,000,000 copies, also describes the effects of bodily changes on the emotions.

He may not manage his new body with as much co-ordination as he used to, and the same applies to his new feelings. He is apt to be touchy, easily hurt when criticised. At one moment he feels like a grown-up and wants to be treated as such. The next he feels like a child again and wants to be cared for.[5]

The feeling of living in two worlds, having grown out of the one and not yet being ready for the other, is put into a sociological consumer context by Dobson:

The self-esteem of an early adolescent is also assaulted in the Western culture by his youthful status. All of the highly advertised adult privileges and vices are forbidden to him because he is "too young". He can't drive or marry or drink or smoke or work or leave home. And his sexual desires are denied gratification at a time when they scream for release. The only thing he is permitted to do, it seems, is to stay in school and read his dreary textbooks.[6]

Dobson, who is writing out of the American context, conceded that the last sentence is an over-statement. But it fairly summarises the feeling of many adolescents. It is a time when they look for support to protect an ego that is threatened in many ways, and to achieve an identity by membership of a peer group to sustain the identity which they feel is in danger of disappearing under an onslaught of changes.

Recreational influences on the adolescent

Such profound changes, both physical and psychological, find an echo in the world of play and imaginative growth. A characteristic of many of the areas we have discussed so far is what I would call a half-way, or truncated, sexuality.

It is characterised by an exploration of sexuality for a market whose experience of sexuality is limited, confused, or at best unfinished. Because not only teenagers read teenage magazines, and because of the notorious discrepancy in maturity and achievement between individuals of the same age in the 10–13 age group, it is not an exploration that is just presented to adolescents.

There are two factors that should be mentioned before we go further, to locate the discussion in a wider context.

First, *young people's magazines are only one of many influences upon them.* Any exploration of sexuality that takes place in a magazine takes its place alongside similar explorations in, for example, soap operas that are watched by a young audience (for example, the positive promotion of homosexuality in *Eastenders*, which originally revolved round a relationship with a young teenager; and the ambiguity of young Paul and Gail Robinson's marriage of convenience in *Neighbours*, where sex was not included in the original contract but was clearly desired by each party, unknown to the other).

Many households have tabloid newspapers, and the page 3 phenomenon affects both boys' and girls' views of adult sexuality; and almost all have television, where many sit-coms and comedy shows flirt with sexuality without ever facing up to it (*The Benny Hill Show*, for example, is all about sex and says nothing about relationships).

So it is important, when looking at young people's magazines, to see that where they present a problem, it is part of a bigger problem. Often critics choose the most visible target, without realising that it is a symptom rather than a cause.[7]

Second, *although many magazines have a formally defined readership of older teens and early twenties, younger children read them too*. The obvious case is that of siblings; a younger brother or sister will pick up and read the magazines of the older child. But it's also true that the age of physical puberty is lowering, and sexual allusions that might have seemed incomprehensible to a child of a certain age two or three decades ago will now strike a familiar chord.

> There is strong evidence that the physical growth of children and teenagers has speeded up over the last 100 years so that the changes of puberty occur faster and earlier today.... It seems that there has been a flattening out of this rate of change [increasingly early menstruation] since the early 1970s.[8]

It would be unwise, therefore, to think that your eleven-year-old son or daughter is not intrigued by magazines and comics designed for much older children.

Safe sex

How then does this 'playing with sexuality' show itself? Most commonly, it is expressed as a mild eroticism, such as is clearly seen in the pop magazines (which are read by children of all ages, including siblings):

> There's one surefire way of telling if your lad's a man or a mummy's boy—just look at his washing line! Yup, it's amazing how much you can discover simply by having a butcher's at his undies.[9]

says *Blue Jeans & Patches*, and illustrates the feature with a picture of four young men stripped to their underpants, hanging washing on a clothesline.

Blue Jeans & Patches has a core readership in the 13–17 year old range,[10] and I am not suggesting that the feature I have mentioned will corrupt most children's minds. It has an element of humour in it, and it is carefully put together. Readers are not urged to remove their boyfriends' trousers to inspect the undergarments, but are told to 'look at his washing line'. The illustration shows four very normal boys, not posed as glamour or as sex symbols, wearing modest boxer shorts. And in any case, if the illustrations were to accurately reflect the text, the boys would not be wearing any underpants at all but hanging them on the clothesline!

But the feature does represent a flirting with sexuality, a playing with the concept of sex as power, presented to a readership that includes young teenage girls. A thirteen-year-old girl is in the process of physical development. A feature like this contributes towards the socialisation of her sexuality before she has had the opportunity to come to terms with it. She is being given formulas and attitudes with which to discuss the subject when necessary. The magazine also plays a small part in conditioning her relationships— one might ask, what is the attitude of her boy friends who may read the magazine? How do those boys then relate to her?

Whether a parent of a particular thirteen-year old would want that child to read *Blue Jeans* regularly is an individual choice. Personally I would not, even though I respect the restraint that is exercised. I believe that the time for young people to have to come to terms with sexual innuendo— even discreet sexual innuendo—is when they are older than their very early teens. Of course they will be exposed to playground talk, sex jokes from contemporaries and older relatives, and the incessant battering of the media anyway; but I would think that damage-limitation where it can be achieved is a sensible move.

A magazine that handles the issue of sex and puberty very well is *Girl* magazine, targeted at an age range of 10–15 years, which puts it squarely in the puberty readership. A magazine with a long and commendable history, it is much more open to discussing topics such as periods and AIDS than its founders were, and it seems to provide a valuable service in giving sensible and straightforward answers to readers who write with problems. Its fiction and features, too, don't attempt to deny the romantic dimension of teenage life.

Both magazines, I would say, are aware of their responsibilities to younger readers, though it was disturbing to find several advertisements in *Girl* from Voiceline, a telephone dial-up service ('Are you a super snog or dishy date? Lip Bumping—what do boys like?').

Boys and girls

The magazines so far discussed are girls' magazines. Boys' magazines are different in a number of ways.

Eagle, now merged with *Mask*, has as long a history as *Girl*, and still runs 'Dan Dare', the story that used to be on its cover—albeit now with inferior artwork, and a scantily-clad woman who would never have been allowed into the old comic.[11]

Women, in fact, play very little part in *Eagle* (they didn't have much of a role in the old one, either). There are no active female characters, and they are absent from many of the stories. As in many other boys' comics, sexual relationships belong to another world, and romance is not a priority.

In some ways, this is understandable. It is not sexist to say that most little boys tend to favour play that celebrates achievement and underplays relationships, whereas little girls tend to hold the two in a better balance.

So the average play school or junior school playground, you will *tend* to see (it is not by any means an inviolable rule) the girls playing together and the boys playing in competition with each other (and if that sounds a sexist assumption, it should be remembered that research indicates that the female IQ stabilises before that of the male!).[12] But a division such as seems to exist between the interests of teenage girls' and boys' magazines may perhaps be expected.

A lack of interest in the opposite sex is not a destructive or imaginatively disabling trait for a teenager, and it could easily be argued that it is an improvement on some of the girls' comics. Unfortunately, the absence of romantic storylines in most boys' magazines does not mean that no attitudes to women are expressed. Quite the opposite is the case.

Front cover raunchiness

Crash is a magazine published by Newsfield, a Ludlow-based company. It is aimed at owners of the Amstrad/Sinclair Spectrum range of home computers, and only covers those computers (a companion magazine, *Zzap!*, covers the Commodore series of machines).

Children of all ages are fascinated by computers, and some pre-teens are highly expert. As a result, the conventional 'core readership' estimate for its readership is probably irrelevant. It provides technical information, which is often quite within the grasp of very young enthusiasts; news of forthcoming products and the computer scene in general; and—for the bulk of the magazine—reviews of games and hints on how to play them.

So its readership encompasses a wide (and largely male) age-range. This makes it more disturbing that a running correspondence has gone on in the magazine for a few years regarding readers' opinion of the acceptability or otherwise of what some readers see as excessive sex and violence in the magazine.

Like most computer magazines, *Crash* regularly provides

complete solutions to computer games, enabling arcade games to be beaten and adventure games to be solved. (It remains an odd characteristic of the computer hobby that people who have paid ten pounds for a game will go out a month later to purchase a magazine that will tell them how to solve it in five minutes.)

Most computer magazines that feature games have a 'tipster' to provide tips and hints. In 1986 *Crash*'s tipster was Hannah Smith. The magazine's readers, and the editorial team, had a running gag on the subject of Miss Smith, with a variety of extremely chauvinistic jokes and word-plays, in which Miss Smith entered enthusiastically.

The August 1986 issue of *Crash* featured a larger than usual tips section. The headline on the full-colour cover said BEAT THE ALIENS WITH HANNAH SMITH'S PLAYING TIPS. The illustration was of an alien in a slime-covered wrestling ring, pinned to the ground by a recognisable likeness of Miss Smith, wearing a leotard and sitting astride the alien. The alien's arm is being pulled between Miss Smith's legs and waved in the air.

It is a very questionable image, belonging more to the world of soft pornography than to the world of magazines that have substantial teenage readerships. The rock star Madonna, for example, was reported as using similar gestures in her stage shows, and it is a common gesture in striptease performances, as the *Daily Mail* critic pointed out:

> Even when she bends down to display her bottom with 'kiss' written across its scarlet satin panties, she has none of Bette Midler's raunchy wit.... And for that matter when she discards these intimate objects, rubbing them provocatively between her legs before tossing them into the audience, she is offering nothing more enticing than your everyday Soho stripper.[13]

Is *Crash*'s cover a pornographic cover? No, it isn't. It is a picture of an alien being defeated in a wrestling ring. But it draws on images which have an erotic content, emphasised by the skimpiness of Miss Smith's costume, the ample bosom which the artist has given her, and the fact that Miss Smith's physical attractiveness has been the subject of running gags in the magazine for a long time.

I doubt very much whether children or young teenagers recognise the identity of some of the images, but there is an appeal being made to their own emerging sexuality which they barely understand.

The August 1986 cover was *Crash*'s most extreme effort. I felt somewhat embarrassed paying for it at the counter of my newsagent (did the assistant know it was a computer magazine—or did she think it was a very different kind of publication?). Covers since then have been more restrained, drawing more on conventional images of violence and less on covert eroticism, and the same criticisms cannot be made of them.

Indeed, as this book was being proof-read, *Crash* changed format, with fewer pages, a much greater emphasis on game-playing and a reduction in technical content, and a free tape containing four computer games of high quality. The level of writing appears to be shifting to a markedly younger reader-ship, and though (at the time of writing) it is too early to be certain, the new *Crash* appears to present fewer problems for concerned parents—though its educational and technical content is much more sparse.

But the older *Crash* represents a type of image still common in boys' magazines. It will not rot a child's soul; but parents and concerned adults may well ask whether it is at all helpful, and what controls there ought to be on how such magazines are distributed.

Playground crudity

Sadly, the trend towards sexual crudeness is accelerating in some computer magazines. *Sinclair User* is an example. This is a review of a game called *Savage*, by John Riglar:

Savage is big. I'm not talking about the film or a certain part of my anatomy (my nose, you pervs!), but *Savage*, the game....[14]

This is fairly typical of Riglar's style. When giving tips on a helicopter game, he can't resist the double-entendres:

Choppa, choppa, choppa (fnar, fnar, fnar).... And now we come to a...battleship which does sod all. (Pardon the language.)...Swept wing fighters will appear directly ahead of your chopper (Ooer).[15]

Notes for readers who haven't been in a playground for a while: 'chopper' is a common euphemism for the male sex organ, 'fnar, fnar, fnar' is intended to represent a dirty laugh, and 'Ooer' is put in to make sure you understand what you're supposed to be sniggering about.

Sinclair User is not the only magazine that uses this technique. I think that there are several aspects that give cause for concern.

1. Most parents are unlikely to have looked closely at the magazines their children are reading

Some parents will assume that computer magazines are high-tech, incomprehensible, and useful for helping their child in school. They will not realise that these magazines are part of adolescent culture, and that computer games have the same transient, 'chart' appeal of the pop music market.

I am not suggesting that every parent whose children read *Sinclair User, Crash* or similar magazines should insist that they stop reading them immediately (impossible to enforce anyway, as the magazines circulate in schools). But good parenting involves having some general idea of what is going into one's children's minds. I am not advocating censorship, but awareness—awareness which can often be the basis for productive discussions between parent and child.

I don't apologise for using the word 'child' in this context. *Sinclair User's* core readership age-group, as defined by their advertising department, is from eleven-years old to eighteen-

years old, with the average reader being aged about thirteen-
and-a-half. However, I was told when I rang the magazine
that their actual readership extends from eight-year olds to
ninety-year olds. This was said humorously, but sibling interest must produce quite a few readers at the lower end of that
scale.

2. Magazines influence children's minds

They put the language of the playground sniggers and
behind-the-bike-shed humour into permanent, printed form
and thereby give it credibility.

It might be argued that children go through phases, that
most bring some playground language into the home, and
that the best way to deal with it is not to make an enormous
fuss about it. As I write, my wife and I are having this
problem with our younger daughter, who has just started
primary school and is prone to devastate the tea-table with
some very odd words and jokes. If one watches her face as
she delivers these bombshells, it is clear she is testing their
effect on us. If we remain calm, she loses interest. Some
children, it should be added, pick up words without having
any idea at all that they are offensive, and can be quite
distressed when they discover this. It is a good idea not to
assume invariably that a child is hoping to shock. He or she
might need a sympathetic chat, in which, perhaps, the
amount of understanding of the new word or joke can be
tactfully gauged.

It might also be argued that the computer magazines are
following a style, and that none of the readers take the
language seriously: that to object to it is to miss the point
entirely and reveal a serious lack of a sense of humour.

But how helpful is it for a child to have a regular diet of
vulgarity, sexual innuendo, double-entendres, and obsessive
interest in bodily functions? Would a parent be happy to
allow a child to spend as much time in the company of people

who actually spoke that way? How happy would that parent be to have such language used at the tea-table?

It is rarely obscene language, more often simply crude or bawdy. But whether it is helpful language for an eleven-year-old or thirteen-year-old to enjoy is doubtful. For Christian parents, who want to bring their children up with some understanding of the deceptive power of the unguarded tongue, it is a very big question indeed.

3. It is language that is destructive to women

The most damaging aspect of this kind of language is that it majors on sex but has nothing to say about relationships. It uses women as the butt of cheap jokes, yet ignores boy-girl relationships. It is a particularly nasty form of male chauvinism, born out of the (inaccurate) assumption that only males are interested in computers.

Frequently girls and women write to the magazines and protest, but their letters, though printed, are few and ineffective.

In a world where women are hurt every day by cheap jokes—and, in exclusively male publications, are reduced to sex objects—it is disturbing to read a magazine like *Your Sinclair*, whose editor, Teresa Maughan, is known as T'zer to her readers.[16] Ms Maughan's desirability is a running gag in the magazine, and there are lots of innuendos (readers whose game-solving tips are printed receive a badge saying 'I've got big tips'). A sample of *Your Sinclair*'s readers' joke column runs:.

> Q. What goes in stiff and dry, comes out limp and wet and gives pleasure to two people?
> A. A teabag![17]

When Page 3 girl Corinne Russell was used as the cover girl for the computer game *Vixen*, featuring a scantily clad woman armed with a whip, *Your Sinclair* screamed from the cover:

SCOOP PREVIEW! Vixen—it'll whip you up to a frenzy! Plus—Your Vixen pin-up inside!

The magazine centrefold featured a pull-out poster of Corinne Russell.[18] The use of the Page 3 model in this way was an endorsement of the entire Page 3 ethos, which an increasing number of women and men find extremely offensive and degrading.

4. By relying heavily on innuendo, it succeeds in cheapening everything it touches

Parents who write to the magazines and object to such things receive short shrift, but a Mrs N McHarg wrote to *Your Sinclair* from Glasgow regarding a reader's letter published in the previous issue:

> This type of smut one would expect to read in the seedier magazines which are mainly displayed on the top shelves of newsagents out of reach of the younger readers, and which I would certainly not have in my home. Do you realise that children of the age 10/11 years old buy this magazine?
> ...I found your reply just as disturbing as that awful letter. Innuendos such as were printed, I can do without having to explain to my son.
> Does it mean that the filthier the letter, the more chance of having it printed or receiving a free game?

(Games are awarded as prizes for the 'star letters'.) Teresa Maughan's reply was as follows:

> Certainly not! The whole point of innuendos is that older readers who understand such things will get the joke, whereas younger ones will not even realise there is a joke. I'm sorry you were offended—but if your son didn't understand, there was nothing to explain. The magazine is aimed at a slightly older age group, though I'm aware younger children read it, which is why we don't print anything explicit.[19]

This is not an adequate answer, and one wonders how much Ms Maughan has watched children together. It is simply not true that children of ten or eleven will not realise the significance of an innuendo. Some will actually be as mature as older children. But even if this is not the case, they will usually know that something is there to be understood, and will try to work out what the joke is.

Arguably, it is *more* damaging to a younger child than an older one, because the younger child spends more time deciphering the joke. In the same way, not printing 'anything explicit' merely doubles the snigger-value of the joke—the tea-bag joke quoted above depends entirely on false expectations aroused by a deceptive innuendo. In any case, there is a great difference between sniggering in the playground and setting up a profitable publishing operation to do the same thing for a readership of thousands on a monthly basis. There is a real exploitation of children implicit here which should make all parents concerned.

5. *The kind of journalism we have been considering is a seed-bed for other problems*

Even in conventional magazine publishing, some of the publications for older teenagers and early twenties venture into some very troubled areas. *Just Seventeen*, in its April 1988 issue, ran a feature on Emma Ridley, the girl who shot to tabloid fame when she married in America at the age of 15. Her exploits as a celebrity included a striptease at a London fashion show, which was widely reported in the newspapers. *Just Seventeen* printed photographs of the strip, the last of which showed her naked apart from a pair of skimpy briefs.

The morality, not to say the legality, of publishing photographs of semi-naked fifteen-year-old girls is dubious. That *Just Seventeen* did is not inconsistent with the rest of the magazine; in the same issue, Melanie McFadyean, the magazine's Agony Aunt, wrote to a fifteen-year-old who was worried because sex with her boyfriend was painful. The answer was ambiguous:

As you know, you are a year under the age of consent, so your boyfriend would be breaking the law by having sex with you, which is all the more reason to get your mother's support, help and approval.[20]

This is not an incitement to break the law, but it is an irresponsibly vague piece of advice to a young teenager.

In Chapter 8 we will be looking at some very unpleasant publications indeed, which represent an entirely different type of problem—explicit pornography—and to which children have ready access. I am not suggesting that any of the magazines we have considered in this chapter are of such a pornographic nature. But the acceptance of sexual sniggering, playground sex-talk, and obsession with sex to the disregard of relationships—which many magazines *do* exhibit—certainly play a part in preparing the ground.

Parental action

What can parents do about the problems I have described in this chapter? I think several steps are necessary.

1. Read the magazines

It is all too easy to let a boy or girl buy a magazine, read it, and discard it without ever looking at it yourself. Evaluate the magazines your children like to read. Some are positively good, some are fairly neutral, others are bad in a number of ways.

2. Look carefully at their non-fiction content

For example, the issue of the advice given to young people in Advice Columns is a much-discussed one. It is certainly important that facts should be available for young people unable to find information from parents, and many children are frightened about their physical development, sexually transmitted diseases, relationship problems and many others.

But in these columns as elsewhere, many messages are being conveyed by implication.[21] That of *Just Seventeen* seems to be 'Do what you like so long as you don't hurt anybody, and don't be intimidated by convention or prejudice.' The lesson for parents and responsible educators is obvious. Straightjacketing is not caring, and every generation has to find an effective way of passing on values, without at the same time shackling the desire of the young to be independent.

Some magazines are helpful in this. But others are not. Many parents have never looked at the magazines that their children and teenagers read. Do so now; you may be shocked.

3. *Understand their appeal*

For many children, the magazines provide peer-group support at a time when, as we saw at the beginning of this chapter, children feel very vulnerable. At a time of physical change and sexual gaucheness, a child appreciates the feeling of banding together with his or her own sex and talking freely about sexual matters. Much of the sex banter in the computer magazines is merely giving the readers a sense of corporate self-confidence in an area where they have little expertise.

4. *Attempt to put into a child's life the balanced teaching which many magazines conspicuously fail to give*

Often an incomplete, truncated view of sex and relationships is given. The only fulfilling sexual experience is that which takes place in the context of a relationship between committed couples. Christians believe that this means marriage, and that sexual intercourse before marriage or outside marriage is ruled out.

This doesn't mean that nothing can be known or appreciated about sex before marriage, or that some kinds eroticism should only enter a person's life at marriage. But that is very different from a magazine using sex jokes as a weapon or as a defence.

5. Consider complaining

You can complain to the editor, the publisher, or the news-agent. We will be looking at this area in more detail later, but here we can emphasise that the magazines appear to adopt the innuendo style *because* they have a younger audience, despite Teresa Maughan's comments quoted above. Magazines with an older readership rarely write in this way. There is no heavy-handed barrage of smut and innuendo in the magazines for the Amiga and Atari ST computers, which are expensive and tend to be bought for older children. Magazines for users of business machines don't write like it, nor do weekly news magazines. The content of the Sinclair and Commodore magazines we have looked at is written at a predominantly childish level because children read them.

Turning the tables

If nothing is given the child to counteract it, a diet of certain computer magazines will give a boy the impression that sex is dirty; a non-stop barrage of innuendo can hardly do other-wise. A diet of certain girls' magazines may well give girls the impression that their sexuality is an instrument of power, to be used to ensnare men. I rang one of Voiceline's numbers advertised in *Girl* and heard a young female voice explain-ing, to any child who cared to dial the number, how to tell if a man had 'got the hots' for you, and how to make sure that he did.

As with many issues discussed in the book, the problem is not that the magazines are a calculated onslaught on Chris-tian values or even family values by a unique interest group. What they represent is a fair reflection of our society.

Parenting is our opportunity to help children grow into that society, without being overwhelmed by it.

The magazines can represent a desensitisation which could well come too early. It is up to us to decide when our children confront the devaluation of sex and relationships that marks the world in which they will have to live. That decision can only be effectively implemented if our caring, our example, and our straightforward teaching about the simple sexual facts speak louder than the sniggers and the knowing, worldly flaunting of female wiles.

7

The First Kid on the Block

Welcome, Young Warriors!

—proclaims Scrollos, writing his regular letter to the readers of the *Masters of the Universe* comic:

> Many of you have sent photographs to me showing your large collections of Masters of the Universe toys. I really enjoy seeing these and have recorded each and every one of them in my Master Computer.[1]

'101 Little Ponies!' announces a My Little Pony Club club page.

> The SWEET CELEBRATIONS LOVING FAMILY can't see themselves in this photo of Kelly Dawn Hinchlife's Little Pony collection! Mummy and Daddy Sweet Celebrations are glad they haven't got so many babies in *their* family, Kelly![2]

Parents facing regular child's pleas on pocket-money day, to be allowed to add yet another collectable to the crammed toy-box, windowsill or dressing table, may well have groaned if they read those items. It's a common characteristic of the comics; children who have amassed large quantities of the featured toy are admired and applauded, and other children are given a gentle nudge to improve the size of their own collections (it is, after all, a very good way of getting your photo in the comic).

A child is rarely content to own just one Little Pony, or a

single He-Man figure, or a single member of a Sylvanian family.

The reason is partly the demands of play, in that when you are trying to recreate the battling factions of the planet of Eternia, the cast is a large one. But that's not the only reason. A stronger one is that the advertising and promotion of toys often carry an underlying message: 'Be the first kid on the block to have the whole set.... Collect the next in the series.... We are about to release a new set of products that you won't want to miss.... Every true fan/champion of the Power/etc will want to add *this* toy to his collection...etc.'

The comics, television shows and videos play a major part in the process. New adventures introduce new characters, and those characters are usually new products which the manufacturers have recently added to their range. As the child acts out the story of the comic, he or she needs the new toy in order to do so.

This actually highlights a deficiency in the whole philosophy of some collectable toys. A toy that is highly detailed and full of specific information can actually *limit* the opportunities for imaginative play, because the toy can only ever be what it has been designed to be ('directed play' is viewed with mistrust by most writers on play). But Kenneth Grahame's rocking horse could double as a gun-boat when necessary.

The detail and complexity of many collectables, on the other hand, is reflected in the variety of accessories that can be bought for them; weapons for He-Man, alien devices for Transformers, riding outfits for Sindy, roller skates for a Little Pony, a bikini for Barbie and many, many more.

It's another characteristic of the toy market. My Little Pony, for example, offers children a sophisticated range of grooming kits, grooming parlours, stables, and lots more. If you collect She-ra, Princess of Power toys, there are books and cassettes available. And so on....

Exploitation?

Parents faced with this never-ending drain on limited resources, and constantly urged to inspect the latest expensive addition to the range of their children's favourite toy, might well feel a grudging admiration for the manufacturers and publicists who seem able to generate a limitless demand and tap an inexhaustible market.

To be fair to the manufacturers, what is happening in the toy industry is standard advertising practice: to convince people who do not need a product that they do in fact need it—very much.

So toy advertising uses all the techniques of advertising to adults.[3] One example is *hype*. A 'hyped' product is one that is given massive exposure and extravagant praise so that it secures a place in the market more by the force of the advertising campaign than by any qualities it might happen to have itself. Anybody watching television advertising at Christmas time will see this working in the toy industry, as toy companies fight for a large share of the enormous profits to be made.

> This Christmas we'll spend £540 million on toys—around £75 for every little Tom, Dick and Harriet. Choice is between techno and trad—state of the art micro-chippery versus cuddly toys. . . .[4]

Glamorisation is also employed: the implication that ownership of a particular toy will allow the child to accompany it into exotic and undreamt fantasy lands. Tropical Barbie and the rock star Jem are two toys that exemplify this.

Many toys are advertised by *promotion by association*. For example, they are shown in the context of an idealised, glossy family, surrounded by material comforts. Buy the toy, it is implied, and this is the sort of world you could enter, because this is the sort of world in which this toy lives. (This is a ploy that Meccano used in the old days, but they made a

major error; the kindly pipe-smoking father was shown helping two enthusiastic boys to build a crane, and there were no
females in sight. Meccano was missing half its potential
audience. Lego's strategy in modern times has been the
exact opposite, with predictable and spectacular results.)

And toys are often advertised by inviting the child who
purchases them to join in a moral crusade—to side with He-
Man, for instance, against the evil Skeletor (though children
who prefer a different allegiance are also catered for):

> Special message from He-Man: "If you want to show that you
> support my fight for good, wear my badge. Just send a stamped
> addressed envelope marked 'He-Man' to the address below, and
> you can count yourself as one of my friends." Hisses Skeletor:
> "To join my henchmen, mark the envelope 'Skeletor', and you
> can share in my power."[5]

Does all this amount to exploitation of children? *Do* advertisers manipulate young people against their will? It's a difficult issue and one that is much debated. But it is fair to say
that advertising to children is not a uniquely dark and evil
plot aimed at our future, that nobody has yet uncovered. It is
simply a collection of techniques very similar to those that
we encounter ourselves in our adult lives (which leaves, of
course, the question of whether it is a good thing to use those
techniques against children at all, and this we will discuss
shortly).

It's in the nature of advertising to manipulate and exploit.
It is a manipulation that we accept, because—rightly or
wrongly—we consider that once recognised, it can be
defeated. And sometimes, for example at Christmas, we are
surrounded by so many advertisements that we are lulled
into thinking that we know all the ways that they are going to
influence us—and our children.

The collecting instinct

It is also fair to say that collecting is a characteristic of childhood. There must be many adult men like myself, who spent much of their childhood dreaming of the next birthday or Christmas which, we hoped, would bring the coveted 'Conversion Set' which would turn our No. 6 Meccano Set into a No. 7 Set.

Brooke Bond picture cards, I-Spy booklets, Dinky Cars and many more of my childhood passions all have their equivalent today; and when I am in a toyshop and overhear a child begging a parent to be allowed 'just one more Little Pony', I recognise the collecting instinct from my own experience.

From that point of view, you could even argue that today's children are more fortunate than we were. There is no ultimate Lego set corresponding to the magnificent and colossally expensive No. 10 Set that waited at the end of the Meccano road, huge and seductive in its polished wooden chest of drawers. (You can still buy it today, for around £700.) Were it not such a yellow-and-silver mockery of its former red-and-green glory, I would be dreaming of owning it even now. I remember a wonderful Christmas week two years ago when I was one of a group of full-grown men, literally kneeling round an opened display No. 10 Set in Hamley's toy store in London. We had never met each other before, but we were united in a common memory of childhood.

But Lego has no such expensive goal. There are the Technical Lego sets, and some boxes are bigger than others, but there is no target as such to reach. And there is an ever-expanding range of My Little Ponies, but no ultimate and exorbitant Pony of Ponies to aspire to.

Most toys today have a sideways rather than a vertical collectability. There will always be new items added to the line, but the cost of the *Star Wars* character you buy in twelve months' time won't be catastrophically more than the one you buy today.

Of course the combined cost of all the individual pieces is a different matter, and presents problems to do both with family finances and also bringing up children with a responsible attitude to possessions in a world where many have very little. But it is some help to parents, I think, that though He-Man has Castle Grayskull and Barbie has a whole plastic house to live in, these are diversions rather than goals in the collecting process.

Pressure and manipulation?

A parent helping a child to come to terms with the pressure to acquire more and more of a favourite toy series is actually working in a very important area of parenting. Many issues are involved and they are all important ones.

For example, many families do not have enough money to go round. Is it fair that Johnny should be allowed to develop a materialistic attitude to possessions early in life, when his parents are trying to teach him about sharing and generosity—all the more vital in a family that is not well off?

In a family that is comfortably well-off, and in which pocket money is adequate and organised, children still need to be taught a responsible attitude to possessions. Is the amassing of large quantities of a particular toy a good thing? Perhaps not, when it is realised that the child who is an obsessive collector of a single toy loses the opportunity for a varied and exploratory play life.

And perhaps not, indeed, when one considers that most of us would like to bring our children up with some understanding of how privileged we are in the West, when 800,000,000 people in other parts of the world are living at or below starvation level.

Consumerism and the big money

Viewed in that light, the sheer amounts of money invested in promoting toys begin to look almost obscene. David Mauer, president of one of the divisions of Kenner-Parker Toys, estimated in 1987 that a full-scale launch of a major toy will cost anything from $5,000,000 to $10,000,000 for advertising, *plus* $12,000,000 to $15,000,000 to produce a television cartoon series featuring the toy. Kenner gives this kind of backing to about six new toys per year.

When the cost of launching can be as much as $25,000,000, the criteria of success are similarly huge. Success is reckoned to be anything in excess of sales of $75,000,000 to $100,000,000 and upwards. Five years earlier, a toy achieving sales of $25,000,000 was considered a hit. But today, it's a tougher market.

> Kenner's Hugger Bunch, a line of puffy-cheeked plush dolls with names like Tickles and Precious Hugs, produced respectable sales after a launch costing "well over $10 million", says Mr Mauer. But at retail prices of around $30, he explains, it was probably overpriced, and sales fell far short of the $70 million to $100 million anticipated by Hallmark Cards Inc., which had licensed the characters to Kenner. The toy company stopped producing the line earlier this year.[6]

Looking at the marketing strategies and the scale of investment, it is impossible not to recognise the battle that is being waged for the hearts of children.

> As Christmas approaches, Barbie, the world's favourite doll, had better abandon her ball gowns and leotards and borrow some heavy duty combat gear from her brother, Action Man. A new doll is on the scene and the average toy box may not be big enough for the both of them.
>
> Hasbro, one of America's largest toy firms, has spent $7m on promoting Maxie, a Californian blonde, who is a direct rival to Mattel's Barbie. Maxie has her own range of accessories to beef up sales, including a $13 'day dreaming bed' and a locker.
>
> Wayne Charness, a Hasbro vice-president, told me that

Maxie's sales performance in the first few months are well in line with projections but insists that she is different from Barbie. "Barbie is a 21-year-old career girl," he sniffs. "What little girls want is a teenager and Maxie fulfils that role." Now that Barbie has her own perfume, though, Maxie will have to do more than day dream.[7]

We have earlier discussed the significance of peer group pressures. These play a part in the commercial battle:

Watching particular television programmes, or having a particular heavily-advertised toy, become important methods of being accepted by other children. The child becomes a kind of prize in the battle waged between competing interests in society.

And when children become teenagers, the peer group—again, often abetted by commercial interests—can become the main influence over a young person, far outweighing other agents of socialisation such as family or school. Teenagers are an important commercial market which did not exist before the 1950s.[8]

We also saw how toy-related magazines and comics influence children, and how effective they are in making children want the featured toys. This is acknowledged by the manufacturers.

Tonka is backing up its top selling girls' range, Keypers, with a massive marketing campaign to make it the bestselling toy this Christmas. A £1 million ad campaign being launched this month coincides with the launch of the first issue of the Keypers magazine.

"The magazine is part of a comprehensive licensing programme," says marketing director Denis Horton. "Fleetway Publications sees it as a way of generating sales and we see it as a way of building up further interest in the product among girls."

Keypers will be challenging Hasbro Bradley's My Little Pony as the bestselling girls' line. My Little Pony also has a girls' comic, said to be a top seller, to support its sales.[9]

Keypers became one of the best-selling girls' toys of 1986. *My Little Pony* magazine is certainly a top seller too. Its circulation in January to June 1988 was 80,330, and that of its companion *My Little Pony and Friends* 47,659. Together they outsell *Care Bears* (54,717 for the same period), *Thundercats* (51,448), *Transformers* (73,789), and most others. Obviously there is a battle worth winning here too, for the affections of children and the pockets if not of the children, then of their parents.

The hard (and soft) sell

These two sides to the issue of obsessive collecting—the fact that it is a natural inclination of children, and the fact that the advertisers enthusiastically feed this inclination with massive funding—are perhaps relatively straightforward.

But advertising has always had an element of deception—after all, if it were not so, advertisements would lose much of their power and effectiveness. Comparatively little toy advertising (or any advertising, for that matter) is a simple statement of the virtues of the product and an invitation to the consumer to choose it in preference to its competitors.

In 1957 Vance Packard coined the phrase 'the hidden persuaders', and illustrated, among other aspects, the effect of advertising on children with quotations like the following from television star Herb Sheldon:

> I don't say that children should be forced to harass their parents into buying products they've seen advertised on television, but at the same time I cannot close my eyes to the fact that it's being done every day.[10]

In attempting to tap the present and future market that children represent, some disturbing and unpleasant techniques are used today to solve the problem defined by Packard as 'marketers...trying to persuade people to buy all the products their companies [can] fabricate'.[11]

Battle of giants

The stakes, in business terms, are often very high. The international toy market in the past decade has been dominated by the struggle between Hasbro (eg My Little Pony) and Mattel (eg Barbie).

Hasbro's success story is remarkable. In the late 1970s the company was losing money; in 1985 it overtook Mattel as number one toy company in the world, with sales of $1.2 billion and profits of $99,000,000.[12] Mattel, which suffered badly when the electronic games market collapsed, has had severe problems in Britain in recent years, for example when sales of the Masters of the Universe line fell from £18,000,000 in 1985 to £4,000,000 by 1987.[13] As I write, Mattel is planning to re-launch the toy at its November 1989 preview. Meanwhile Hasbro's 1987 sales income has been declared as $1.3 billion.

Mattel is suffering the effects of a well-known feature of childhood, which Hasbro has managed to overcome: the tendency for children's toy interests to go in and out of fashion. In most toy companies, a high proportion of its products have to be replaced every year because children simply do not want to play with them any more and the market for that particular toy virtually disappears. Masters of the Universe seems to have gone into a natural decline, whereas My Little Pony goes on and on.

The toy industry doesn't operate in a vacuum. Electronic games, for example, which were the start of Mattel's problems, began to look very poor value for money when you could get a whole home computer for £200 or so. Educationalists, too, found little to commend in such games, whereas computers now have an established place in British schools.

But other factors in the commercial world have helped Mattel as much as Hasbro; for example, the heavily Christmas-dominated toy-sales year has changed since the arrival of huge toy supermarkets such as Toys 'R' Us, so that in 1985 Hasbro shipped almost half its orders in the first part of the year.[14]

So how has Hasbro achieved its success? In a number of ways. First, there is real flair in creating toys which will appeal to children. However one might argue about the educational or other value of the toys, hundreds of thousands of children find them absorbing and addictive. This is achieved by a reliance on almost intuitive judgements and experience gained from past successes. Second, they provide for a child from infancy through to teenage years, from cuddly toys through to board games, so that they can tap the whole child market. Third, they market aggressively, and they understand the power of diversification. Buying a Hasbro toy is only the beginning of the purchase. Your Little Pony will need friends, a stable, a grooming parlour, a straw hat, even roller skates.... And the range includes a mix of pocket-money items and also very expensive toys, so the child can both use his own spending power and influence his parents' much greater resources.

Techniques of the hard sell

In this billion-dollar war for supremacy (Hasbro's declared ambition is to double its market share), the children are the resource which makes it possible. And it is a characteristic of multi-national companies that the survival of the company, rather than the merits of the product, is often the dominating force on management. A major drug company, for example, will certainly have relief of human suffering as the aim of its product; but the aim of its day-to-day business will be to stay in business and capture as much of the market as possible. And there have been well-publicised stories of medical companies that have appeared to exploit the needs of their customers.

It is the parent's responsibility, where toy marketing is concerned, to look especially closely at the way toys are marketed, because their children are not just bystanders who might be attracted to a product. They are a target, upon whom very sophisticated techniques are being practised.

Buying through the box

An example of this is the relationship between toys and television advertising.

One well-known advertising technique is called *product placement*. It is essentially a system of endorsement. Where characters in certain films—often with a large youth following—are seen using a named commercial product (drinking beer, eating a brand of food, etc), that product is there for a reason. Its manufacturers have outbid other manufacturers for this lucrative and extremely low-key product exposure.[15]

It is a short step from there to making the whole film an advertisement—by making the product being sold into the main characters of the film. And a number of advertisers have taken that step. If you visit your local video library you will see the increasing number of films based on toys: *The Care Bear Movie, My Little Pony, He-Man*, and others, all acting as feature-length advertisements. And we have already seen how *My Little Pony* magazine, for instance, disguises advertisements for new products as stories about the arrival of a 'new friend' into pony-land.

Such films and magazines contain a level of advertising that is often unnoticed, but which has proved very effective. The vulnerability of children in the face of sophisticated advertising techniques has prompted considerable argument over the subject in Britain, where product placement, for example, is strongly opposed. However, American films that use the technique are often shown on British television, and there are a number of regular toy-based programmes.

The effects go beyond the mere exploitation of the child's (or parent's) wallet. As Peggy Charren of the American organisation Action for Children's Television has pointed out,[16] such programmes displace other kinds. There are no non-fiction programmes based on toys, no music or live drama.

An example that aroused considerable interest in Britain and America when it appeared in 1986 is *Thundercats*.

> The BBC autumn television schedule of children's programmes includes an American-produced cartoon series, *Thundercats*, that is the subject of a complaint to the US Federal Communications Division.
>
> The Commission is investigating claims that the series is a "programme-length commercial" created primarily to sell toys, and is deciding whether it should carry a disclaimer to that effect.
>
> Miss Anna Home, head of children's programming for the BBC, said yesterday that *Thundercats* was "good, well made entertainment".
>
> But...Mrs Peggy Charren...warned British parents that allowing their children to watch *Thundercats* could result in demands for toys that would cost "hundreds of pounds".
>
> Toys based on characters in the series are available in British shops.[17]

It is not always simply a matter of commercial manipulation. In a market heavily dominated by fantasy, science fiction, and the 'eternal battle against the forces of evil', advertisers often produce material that causes concern on the grounds of needless violence and horror content.

In 1987 Tonka launched a new toy line, called Supernaturals. The storyline was that two half-brothers in ages past fought to rule a kingdom. They became the Supernaturals, ghostly beings that can become powerful creatures. The toys representing the creatures (three good, three evil) can change personality by means of a hologram device incorporated in the toy. They wield glow-in-the-dark weapons, and have the Ghostlings (four good, four evil) as companions and helpers. There is a range of accessories and printed story-matter support. The Supernaturals Tomb of

Doom playset incorporates a very sophisticated hologram, which allows 'entry to the ghost world' by revolving a coffin.

Tonka's Sales Director, Peter Boyle, announced: 'For the first time children have a technological back-up for their fantasies, yet one which in no way impairs their imagination.' A major TV advertising campaign 'to exploit the inherent appeal of holograms' was planned for August and September, which would promote the whole range of Supernaturals toys. But matters did not go as planned.

> Tonka Europe is the latest company to face objections to its advertising from the IBA.
>
> The company's TV commercial for its Supernaturals range of hologram toys, launched in August, has been hit by what appears to be an IBA clampdown on advertising.
>
> The IBA has objected to the commercial on the grounds that the advertisements are far too frightening and macabre for a children's toy.
>
> ... Following the first burst of advertising in August, letters of complaint led to a change in scheduling by Saatchi with a move from a TV-am slot to one in afternoon viewing time.
>
> After a second burst in October, and further complaints, Saatchi says that it actually changed the content of the ad to run a less frightening commercial.[18]

'In the end,' reported *Which?* magazine in December 1988, 'the company stopped showing them.'[19]

The regulations and codes of practice for advertising are very detailed (see Chapter 10). And there are constraints on explicit advertising of toys: in the pre-Christmas period of 1985, for example, TV-am voluntarily undertook to restrict the amount of toy advertising specifically directed at children, and in January 1986 the ITV companies agreed that programmes featuring toys and advertisements offering those toys for sale should not be screened on the same day as each other.

Nevertheless, advertising in its explicit and its concealed forms remains one of the most powerful messages our children will ever receive. As parents, we need to be aware of this, because our reaction needs to be more than a mere willingness or refusal to purchase the toys that are being advertised. We need to understand that our children are vulnerable, and that they are targets for an industry that is aggressively marketing its products.

Toys that shoot back

An example of the involvement of big business in children's imaginative play is the interactive television saga. I use the word 'saga' because it was a long-running complicated chain of events that at times was worthy of a soap opera.

The subject first began to be widely discussed in 1987, when Mattel and Axlon, another Californian company, both announced plans to produce Autumn toys that could be controlled by signals contained in television programmes produced by the manufacturers.

> The special television toys cannot make the new toys play by themselves. Instead, the toy and television programme combine as a shoot-em-up video game, where the child fires at the television set.... Mattel's Captain Power toys include jet fighters, costing about $35, that will fight enemies on the *Captain Power and the Soldiers of the Future* television programme, which is produced by Mattel.... Children fire at the screen from up to three metres away, scoring points when they hit enemy targets. On-screen planes zoom directly at the viewer, and fire back. Children lose points when the enemy hits them. If their score drops to zero, their jet ejects its cockpit.[20]

Axlon's toy, Tech Force, was similar in concept but more complicated: described as a '3-D video gaming system', it comprised two control consoles, each of which controlled up to eight small robots. Two children could pit their small armies against each other, or one child could play against an army controlled by signals coming from a television cartoon.

In some ways it seemed a very exciting development, even

increasing the interactive nature of television and spectator, and so reducing the temptation to sit watching whatever is on the screen. But critics were not slow to point out the disturbing possibilities. Axel's toy cost $250, putting it well out of pocket-money range, but Mattel's prices were low enough to cause real problems for parents whose children were the only ones on the block who didn't have the toy.

A further criticism was that it brought the highly persuasive, compelling world of TV drama into even closer contact with the vested interests of advertisers. And what would the programmes offer for the child who did not own the toy? Making the story irrelevant to such children is actually a very powerful form of advertising—parents will be pressured by their children to buy. And even more disturbing possibilities include that of educational TV, the only children having access to which being those whose parents can afford the electronic gadgetry.

Some of these concerns were expressed in Britain in February 1987, when Peggy Charren, head of Action for Children's Television, an American group, spoke at a London Conference on Television and the Family.[21]

The toy hit problems in Britain. In February 1988, it was reported that ITV had rejected the film series.

Mattel Toys is being forced to launch its controversial interactive toy, Captain Power, in the UK without support from its complementary interactive national TV series. The Independent Television Association has refused to buy the series from the US programme makers, and as yet no ITV company has bought it to show outside children's viewing hours. The ITVA says the children's committee, which chooses the programmes to be bought for children's TV, decided against taking the programmes because they broke new ground in the relationship between TV and toys.... One insider says, "We were uncertain what would happen if two children were watching and one could take part with a toy and the other couldn't afford to."[22]

By June, Mattel in Britain was feeling the effects of the drop in sales of the Masters of the Universe series.

> Toy company Mattel UK has slashed its workforce by a tenth and laid off marketing director Tim Lee in a major redundancy programme introduced because of flagging sales.... Mattel's products include Barbie, Masters of the Universe and the much-hyped Captain Power.... Mattel will now abandon TV advertising for Captain Power.[23]

By September, when Captain Power was first screened in America, interactive television was being seen in Britain as a major threat.

> Millions of children in their own sitting rooms join in intergalactic warfare with Lord Dread and his Bioreds. The youngsters fire at the screen. And the screen fires back. A nightmare vision of the 21st century? No. America today. And if the toy manufacturers get their way, Britain won't be far behind.
>   ...A spokeswoman for ITV's children's committee said: "We have seen a demonstration and decided not to proceed with it."...And the BBC said: "We are not making any decision until we see a completed series."[24]

And by October, Hasbro had abandoned its own attempts to benefit from Mattel's hard work:

> Hasbro Inc. has ended its efforts to develop an interactive video entertainment system. Chairman Stephen Hassenfeld said the effort had produced "unique technology" but because of the high cost of memory chips and other factors, the systems could not be made at a marketable price.[25]

It looks as though British television will not have interactive programmes, along with their problems, for the foreseeable future.

Future trends

But this does not mean that children will not be exposed to those problems in other ways. The Captain Power series was bought by Super Channel satellite TV, and Channel 5 Video has bought the rights to the series. With British television facing a whole new future, and BBC and ITV losing their traditional controlling influence, it may well be that children in the near future will have the material available to them.

In addition, television and video games are changing. Currently games consoles such as the Sega and its more elaborate companion the Konix are entering the market. The concept of a play environment, with real airplane controls instead of a computer joystick and a combat chair to sit in instead of sitting at the kitchen table, is quite close to the concept of Axlon's Tech Force. And with the prices of new technology dropping all the time, who knows whether games that now seem prohibitively expensive might not come within pocket-money range?

Putting things right

The advertisers themselves have conceded that the vulnerability of the child is something that must be respected. But they also argue that the risk to children has been exaggerated. Peter Brown, Manager of Tomy UK Ltd, has pointed out that the amount of advertising of toys has actually diminished, and that one of the effects of advertising has been to reduce the price (in real terms) of successful toys.[26] On toy-related programmes, Ian McMurtrie, Managing Director of Mattel UK, has this to say:

> The media and minority pressure groups would have the consumer believe that toy companies have complete control over the product and scheduling of toy-related TV programmes. The reality is somewhat different....
>
> A TV series does improve awareness of a toy concept, but if a product isn't up to scratch it will not be purchased. Children are quite shrewd enough to know the difference....
>
> In defence of toy-related series I would say many are of excellent quality and have contributed to the improved standards of children's programming.[27]

Yet this model of the child objectively weighing the virtues and drawbacks of a particular toy, measuring every purchase against some predetermined criterion of excellence, is a novelty both in the literature of childhood and in the experience of parents and teachers.

Most writers who have talked about children have indicated that choices are made according to a number of criteria; and in this instance value-for-money and quality may well not be the dominant ones (though children tend to identify and dislike brands of toys which break or come to pieces easily). And any parent who has ever gone shopping with a child will know that many purchases are made on impulse, out of a desire to have the same toy as a friend, because of some peripheral factor such as attractive packaging—or, quite often, because the child has just been given pocket-money and is desperate to spend it.

Of course children are capable of discrimination and of distinguishing between fact and advertisement. But to imply that a child will never—or even rarely—be persuaded, by the allure of a TV feature, to buy a poor-quality toy is over-optimistic.

It is necessary for each parent to decide whether or not their particular children are able to deal with the pressures of advertising. But it's essential to do so in the awareness that the motives of the advertisers often have much more to do with profit than with the needs and personalities of children.

8

The Seduction of the Innocent

By typing in a simple code, a Sunday Times reporter was able last week to choose from a selection of British and American pornography. Within minutes, we saw close-up colour photographs of a couple having intercourse and a demonstration of oral sex.

Sunday Times, *12th March 1989*[1]

I make no apology for borrowing Frederic Wertham's title. There is ample evidence that a large number of children in Britain today are being exposed to explicit, often perverted pornography of a type that far exceeds the largely symbolic representations of sex and violence in the comics against which Wertham campaigned.

How do children have access to this material? Is there a loophole in the sex shops legislation? Have they found a way to borrow hard-core videos from their local video shop? Are pornographic magazines and videos being passed round the playground?

None of these is the case. Anybody, of any age, can obtain the material provided he or she owns a computer and a device called a 'modem' for coupling it to the telephone lines, and knows the telephone number of a bulletin board carrying pornography.

Bulletin boards

A bulletin board is a program run on a computer equipped with a large amount of storage capacity. Usually the operator is a private individual, and the system is run over the normal telephone lines. The computer is left running the program, which is able to receive telephone calls, accept data and store it.

The purpose is, as the name suggests, to be placed where people can leave messages for other people, read messages that have been left for them, and post information, news, and any data they wish to place at other people's disposal. For example, a bulletin board I have used has sections devoted to particular computers, a games section where users can load games over the telephone into their own machines, various multi-player games where players telephone their moves and receive information about what other players are doing, and several other sections.

Without doubt bulletin boards are one of the most enjoyable aspects of computing. When my word processor developed a fault, I mentioned it on a bulletin board, and within hours several people sent the solution to my problem to the board. It's a place where people 'meet' fellow enthusiasts or fellow professionals.

Some can be contacted just by dialling a number; for others, you have to register with your name and address; for a few commercial ones, there is a fee and a charge per call. Because of their ease of use, there have always been problems. In 1983 some bulletin boards which had set up joke sections had to weed them drastically as the bad taste and bad language escalated.

However, this remained a minor theme, and when I included a chapter on home computers in *Children at Risk* in 1986, I identified the most serious risk at being that of crippling phone bills. The situation is very different today.

Pornography by phone

In *Children at Risk*, I mentioned a 'visually quite detailed' computer strip poker game. At that time I had in mind the version running on the Sinclair Spectrum and Commodore 64 machines, which were among the most popular. The graphics on both computers severely limit the amount of detail that can be shown, and the dangers to children were more that they were being introduced to the *concept* of soft pornography than that they were actually experiencing pornography itself.

Today, things are very different. The Atari ST and Amiga computers have dropped in price, and are now taking their place as the top home computers. Both have high-resolution graphics, a subtle range of colours, and impressive sound. It is quite possible to reproduce on the screen of either an image that approaches the quality, if not of a television picture, then at least of the average tabloid photograph.

An example of what is available is the game *Teenage Queen*, from Infogrames, a French-based company.

> You both begin with 100 credits. Once you get the girl's balance below zero she takes off an item of clothing in exchange for some cash. A very flirtatious and sexy teenager, at first you think she's just teasing but she strips off completely if you keep up a winning streak.... Occasional giggles, moans and snatches of speech (mostly in French) have been thrown in for added realism.[2]

The game costs slightly under £20, which might seem to put it out of reach of all but the most prosperous children. But a dismaying amount of computer software changes hands illegally, and the latest games are often circulating, as 'pirated' copies, among circles of friends and acquaintances. The complicated protection schemes devised by the programmers to prevent illegal copying are taken as a challenge by the pirates, and few games escape being successfully 'cracked'.

It is therefore very likely that many young people, and quite possibly some younger children, have copies of the game. The (fully dressed) screen photographs which accompany the review quoted above are very detailed; the details of the card decorations can be clearly seen.

Commercial games, however much they veer in the direction of soft pornography, are clearly controlled by the obscenity laws; moreover, no responsible bulletin board operator would permit a pirated copy to be posted on his board for other users to obtain illegal copies.

A very different situation exists with privately written software, often circulating on small bulletin boards which are not advertised and are known and used by the few who are in the know.

Invaders

I have in my possession a game called 'Astrotit'. It is based on Space Invaders, the classic game in which the player fires at wave after wave of descending aliens. In this version, the player's weapon is an erect male penis. The player fires by lining up the penis with a target and presses the fire button. The 'bullets' are sperm. The targets are female breasts, descending from the sky.

When the player has destroyed a certain number of breasts, play moves on to the next stage. This involves aiming the ejaculated sperm at wave after wave of Bibles descending from the sky.

The game was given to me by a member of my church, because he knew that this book was being written. It had been downloaded from a bulletin board. It was written for the IBM personal computer, a machine that is in thousands of homes. The bulletin board was accessible from the ordinary domestic telephone service, and there was nothing to stop a teenager who had obtained the number from collecting the program and adding it to his or her collection.

At the moment there are very few restraints upon the programmer[3] to stop him or anybody else distributing his program. Yet it is clearly grossly offensive to many people, is particularly offensive to Christians, and is a program that certainly ought not to be available for young teenagers.

Software exchange

The interest in soft pornography extends to several different computers (one manufacturer's computer is not normally able to run a program written for another's). We have an Amiga computer at home which we use as a second office machine and also as a games machine. There is a thriving software exchange community for the Amiga, in which programs on which the author has not claimed copyright are distributed and swapped between Amiga users. I was given a disk among several others which originated, I think, from an Amiga Users' club. It was called 'Every Inch a Lady', and featured a lady with an 84-inch bust. From the accompanying text—an account of her life to date—it seemed that her bust measurement really amounted to a physical handicap, and that it had caused her embarrassment and distress.

The programmer, however, used the text—superficially an appeal for compassion on the part of the viewer towards a women so afflicted—to string together a set of photographs which enabled the viewer to gloat over her body, reproduced in detailed shades of grey on the Amiga screen.

The programmer ended his efforts with a promise. He had lots of other photographs—including some of the model in her early teens—and, if there was enough interest, he would be willing to put together another disk.

Soft porn

This material is available to young people, through normal swapping activity and by downloading from certain bulletin boards. It is also likely that children at school are able to access the bulletin boards through school facilities, where these are unsupervised.

Should anyone doubt that swapping programs is widespread, the rapid penetration of computer 'viruses' in the computer community should confirm it—viruses (rogue programs that corrupt data and cause malfunctioning of the computer) are spread largely by software exchange. Should anyone doubt that young people are involved, the *Sunday Times* article quoted above will provide evidence.

> One list, compiled by a 16-year old computer operator and his father who works for British Telecom, offered us nearly 100 titles, such as Raw Sex, and Madam Fifi's Whore House Adventure. Others portrayed scenes of group, oral and gay sex. [The operator] and his father, 47 , who operate the bulletin board from their family home in Bradford, compiled the list simply by 'downloading' material from other British and foreign bulletin boards and adding it to their own. Similar scenes in magazines would be illegal.[4]

The availability of such material to young people has also worried some of the people involved in this area:

> Porn-for-micros is now on-line. A Birmingham-based bulletin board called "Murdoch's hangout" provides a screen-sex service for anyone wishing to log on.
>
> The service includes digitised pictures and stories of the kind usually found on the top shelf at the newsagent's.
>
> [The operator]...told *Datalink*: "There's a bit of everything. Girls, couples, but no gays. Maybe some lesbian stuff."
>
> ...What does worry [him] is that there is no age verification for new users. Anybody with a modem could log-on. "We're talking about a few people who could be corrupted by this."[5]

This is not a development that has sprung entirely out of nothing. Over the past few years there have been several programs which have had sexual themes, and some, like Infocom's *Leather Goddesses of Phobos*, have acquired cult status for their sexual fantasising.

The program mentioned in the *Sunday Times* report mentioned above, *Madam Fifi's Whore House Adventure*, was included on a disk of Christmas games issued at Christmas 1986 by a reputable software house in association with a respected business computing journal. Though *Madam Fifi* is (a) a game so badly written that most players will lose patience before getting very far with it, and (b)—to judge by the program listing—crude to playground level rather than soft pornography, it was irresponsible of the software house to include it on a disk which was likely to be left unattended in family situations over Christmas.

Sick humour

Possibly more worrying is the rise of sick and vicious software humour. Circulating quite freely in the IBM computer community at present is a game which involves catching babies which are leaping out of a burning building. The player is represented by two firemen trying to catch the babies in a stretcher and put them in an ambulance. Of course it is impossible to catch them all, and most crash to the ground. The graphics are not particularly impressive, but the concept is cynical and sick.

A very sick racist game that originated in Scotland was produced by a group of pirates who illegally altered an existing product. (It should be emphasised that the original game, *Sidewinder*, contained no racist or otherwise offensive matter whatsoever.)

> The game is a mutated version of Mastertronic's *Sidewinder* with the new name of *Paki Bash*. Gamers are apparently urged to kill members of the ethnic community. Police are currently investigating the matter with a view to prosecute under the 1936 Public Order Act.[6]

> The aim for the player, called Ku Klux Joe, is to kill Pakistanis. A screen message states: "Your job is to wipe the bastards out of existence."[7]

A letter to *Computing* magazine pointed out that the problem extends beyond Britain.

Computer enthusiasts may have been horrified to see the recent press revelations about the expanding market in West Germany for neo-Nazi computer games. These games, which are in fact illegal in West Germany, encourage racial hatred and hatred of foreigners, and urge that the country should be purged of beggars, Jews, homosexuals, ecologists and communists. Their spread has been much encouraged by the growing use of home computers.... Young people, who often play these games with such unedifying titles as "Clean up Germany" and "Hallo, Nazi" in the privacy of their bedrooms, are exposed to very evil influences.[8]

If such games are not already circulating in Britain, it is only a matter of time before they are. Importing them is as simple as picking up a telephone and dialling.

Sick magazines

Sick and vicious humour is not, of course, restricted to computer games. It is visible in the High Street. For example, the magazine *Scream!* is the thin end of a disturbing wedge.

Scream! wallows in spookiness. Its holiday specials are full of gruesome effects, and the covers drip blood. Faceless skeletons, mad witches and haunted children appear in its pages, and the whole thing is designed to make the reader cringe with delicious fear—'Be warned! It's the creepiest Special ever!'[9]

The magazine is responding to children's natural inclination for the eerie and macabre, and is successful as a comic because it pushes the limits of fear beyond what a child is used to. Of publications of its type, it is fairly innocuous in some ways and even at its most disturbing it hardly stands comparison with most of the things we have been considering so far in this chapter.

Its major problem is that there is a brutality and a bleak despair about many of its storylines; they exploit the traditional devices of horror, but do not retain its contact with the world of living, loving human beings (the tragedy of *Jekyll and Hyde* and *The Fly*, by contrast, is not so much the horrors that they became, but the fact that they could never return to the world of ordinary people).

A very different comic is *Viz*. This is sold in newsagents, and is very popular—it sells half a million copies every eight weeks. Its images break all the taboos of conventional society. 'The Queen is a bloody cheat!—claims Fulchester man', announces the cover of one edition,[10] and, in the top corner, another story: 'How to have sex with a vampire.' The cartoon stories inside include a series called 'Johnny Fartpants', about a man afflicted with wind, and 'Buster Gonad' about a man whose sex organs are gigantic. There is a particularly unpleasant strip about an axe murderer.

Viz is clearly parodying the comic form itself.[11] It also has something to say about the nature of taboos in society. But that is the same argument used by the libertarian lobby about video nasties;[12] and it is not possible to accept it for its own sake. It cannot be separated from the issue of responsibility towards children.

I find *Viz* extremely distasteful, and I do not believe that it is necessary, if one wants to criticise our taboos on sex and bodily functions, to go so destructively far in the other direction. Nevertheless, I would defend the right of adults to have the right of free speech—were it not for the risk to children.

I bought my copy of *Viz* in my local newsagent's. It was on a lower shelf, about six inches away from the *Beano* and *Dandy*. My daughter was with me. If I hadn't spotted it first and picked it up, she might well have done so. On the cover, it says: 'Not for sale to children'. But in that newsagent's, and many like it, a child could have browsed through undisturbed without having to buy it.

Whatever the sociological and intellectual merits of a

publication such as *Viz*, its right to be freely available to all and sundry is in direct conflict with the rights of children not to be exposed to it at an age where it can do no conceivable good, and could well do harm. Parents should be entitled at least to have the magazine treated like *Playboy* and similar publications in the newsagents: placed out of reach of children on the top shelves.

These are some of the background factors to the new computer pornography. There are many others. One could have mentioned the rise of interest in the occult in recent years, fed by the media and supported by a growth in organised satanism and occult practices—it is claimed that there are 600,000 practitioners of occult arts in America,[13] and there are frequent reports of increasing interest in the occult from young people, especially in the South of England.

Doing something about it

Much of what we have discussed in this chapter is a police matter. There is a clear need for new legislation to cover the specific possibilities of computer pornography, but existing legislation can be used to secure convictions against the distributors and authors of the software. If your child, or a child you know, has access to hard-porn material, or even knows it is circulating in school, you should contact the police.

Your child may have pornography he or she did not ask for: my copy of Astrotit shared a disk with a computer file archive program which took up far more space. Some of the software available involves innocuous titles, and a child could easily get hold of a copy without realising it was pornographic (think of all the businessmen who ordered a Christmas games disk and found they had bought *Madam Fifi's Whore House Adventure*). So if you find such software in your child's possession, don't jump to conclusions.

But the people who do know exactly what they are handling are the people who run the pornographic bulletin boards, software pirate clubs, and user groups dealing in such programs. The only way to crush this new plague is to strike at its distribution centre.

Where soft pornography is involved, there are two parallel needs. One is to approach the distributor as a citizen, requesting that material offensive to many adults and unsuitable for children should be kept out of general view, if it must be stocked at all. The other is the need to mobilise public opinion to back up the initial request. There is a comprehensive action programme on pornography, called Picking up the Pieces, available from CARE Trust (see Chapter 10).

A parent who has a good relationship with their child will be able to talk about most things. But that involves making time to talk, and being genuinely interested. It tends to be the lonely people who are obsessed with pornography, for it often takes the place of loving relationships in their lives. It is part of the task of parenthood to create a channel of communication, and a family relationship—whether it be a conventional family, or a single-parent family, or a three-generation family, or another kind again—that is strong enough to crowd out the competing attractions of pornographic, sick and vicious amusements.

Finally, we can pray. The new pornography is an evil attack on a whole generation of young people. To obtain such material before would have been impossible for most children. Now it is much easier. A door has been opened, and evil and irresponsible people have rushed to use it. Ultimately, the only defence against this threat is the power of prayer. For many of us, it is all we can do. But there is no more effective response to the evil that waits at the end of the telephone line.

9

War Toys, and Christian Options

Christmas should be about loved ones and families, glad tidings
and goodwill to all mankind and, above all, peace on earth.
That, my dears, is what Christmas is all about.

And, still nodding agreement, you know what most of us do
then? To honour the Prince of Peace, the man who said suffer
the little children to come unto Me, we rush out and buy our
little children the instruments of war and sudden death. Rubber
swords, plastic daggers, throwing knives, rifles, hand grenades,
helmets, games to do with skilful killing and, above all, tons and
tons of guns.

Jill Tweedie[1]

When I am discussing toys with any group of parents, one
question is almost bound to come up sooner or later: 'What
do you think about guns and war toys?'

The question is asked in a variety of ways. Some parents
are concerned because they claim that their child is more
aggressive, naughty, or discontented after playing with war
toys. Some have problems with the various scenarios that are
presented with the toys, imagining future wars between
modern-day powers and possibly conditioning children to
expect wars as inevitable. Some have more intellectual problems; their children don't seem adversely affected by playing
with guns, but they are unhappy about all the connotations
that go with that type of play.

It is a question that causes many parents concern. But it is also a question with many facets, and an easy answer isn't possible.

Play and conflict

Inherent in competitive play is the idea of conflict. In a game of chess, the players attack and defend, and each tries to penetrate the defences of the other. In Snakes and Ladders, the fun is in seeing your opponents fall as you rise; there would be little point in playing on your own. When you play football, you are part of an army, marching out to combat with another, equal army.

Of course such games are not seen as war games—though chess probably began as a Persian battle game, and football is in a long line of competitive games reaching back to the first Olympic games, where the young men of Sparta practised the arts of war. But such origins are lost in the mists of time, and people usually regard the games as being quite separate from soldiering and fighting.

Yet an interesting question emerges. If the military origins of chess are so old that the game has lost its warlike nature, what about a board wargame such as *Caesar*[2], which describes a battle during the Gallic Wars, well out of present-day mind and memory?

As a military boardgamer myself (it is only fair to reveal my personal interest in this discussion) I would find it very difficult, if not impossible, to play a game such as that brought out by Mayfair Games on the Falkland War. I live near Portsmouth, and I know people who sailed with the Task Force. I was the ghost-writer of the Vicar of Port Stanley's autobiography. I sat in the evenings and listened to Ian MacDonald's sombre voice detailing the day's casualties. There is no way that I could now while away an hour or two playing a game about the Falklands War, however educational or brilliant a simulation it might be.

But ought one to feel the same about Caesar's Gallic

War? The people who fought are long vanished. But the campaign remains of absorbing historical interest, and a wargame—more accurately, a simulation—is a better way of understanding it than reading most books about it. But if the Gallic War is acceptable, and the Falkland War isn't, then at what point in history *do* wars become acceptable subjects for games? The Second World War? The First? Waterloo?

Another strand in the debate is the argument for war games as surrogate, the argument being that those who play them are sublimating their aggressive instincts. The most famous advocate of this position was H G Wells, who wrote one of the classics of wargaming, *Little Wars* (he played with model soldiers, whereas a board wargamer uses a map and counters; but Well's method is the older). And Wells was a pacifist.

It's an ongoing debate in the wargaming press. 'I am really trying to understand,' wrote a correspondent to the Avalon Hill Game Company's magazine *The General*:

> I simply cannot conceive of making pain, terror, confusion, tragedy, widespread death and destruction, the narrow philosophy of violence in response to violence, a subject of a few hours of "short enjoyment".

A member of Avalon Hill's staff replied:

> Like many non-wargamers, Mr Williams confuses interest in an event with approval of that event. Manifestly, a playgoer need not approve of patricide or incest to appreciate a performance of Oedipus Rex; so why must a wargamer approve of war?[3]

However, wargaming is predominantly a hobby of late teens and upwards; fantasy role-play games have become industry leaders for the younger children. And for most pre-teenagers, wargames are much more physical, and involve acting out the aggression and violence.

Weapons of war

The argument is often used that children, and especially boys, will be aggressive whatever you do, and war toys and guns simply give them the symbolism to act out their aggression. Dorothy Einon regards gun-play as something that children copy from other children:

> If your child is exposed to it, there is nothing you can do. Children are great conformists, taking more and more of their values from their peers as they grow up.[4]

She points out that early gun-play is a fantasy, that the child has no thoughts of really killing, and that children who have fought each other with toy guns all morning will be friends when it is over—unlike adults.

Bruno Bettelheim, whose views on war incline to pacifism, sees war games in children as the proper place to work out once and for all the aggressive traits which in adults lead to war:

> Because I am deeply committed to the conviction that it is high time we dispensed with our archaic heritage of war, I believe that not only as a race (we do not seem to be succeeding well on that front) but as individuals we ought to work through all these primitive remnants within ourselves, so that we may be free of them. This is just what war games can achieve for a child.[5]

The child who makes a gun out of a stick or out of Lego and pretends to shoot another child, is, in Bettelheim's view, *reducing* the possibility of later warmongering rather than increasing it.

The problem, I believe, really begins when the gun the chid plays with is not a stick or a lego brick, but a full-scale, finely-detailed replica of a Kalashnikov rifle or some other miracle of modern warfare. The detail restricts the opportunities for play. The stick that was a gun this morning can be a golf club or a flagpole this afternoon; but the gleaming Kalashnikov can only ever be what it is, a super-efficient killing machine. As the Peace Pledge Union point out in their leaflet *Toying with War*,[6] what would you do with such a toy but point it at people and pull the trigger? That is all you *can* do with it.

I would want to make a very clear distinction between the weapons a child creates for himself (and may later take apart to make something else with the materials), and those that are provided.

Clamping down on war toys

In recent years there has been a major restriction of war toys in a number of places.[7] September 1988 saw the first International Day of the Destruction of War Toys. Malta has banned the import of war toys, and Greece has banned their advertising on television. It is now a criminal offence to import some violent computer games into the Federal Republic of Germany.

The Peace Pledge Union has launched its 'Children and War' project, and sells badges for children to wear bearing slogans like 'War toys are silly', 'Play at peace not war', and 'No more war toys for me'.

In the computer press there is much discussion of war games such as 'Silent Service', in which the player is the commander of an American World War II Submarine, whose task is to sink as many Japanese ships as possible.[8] It is certainly true that many young players of computer games are receiving a regular reinforcement of the view that the Russians are the great enemy, biding their time and waiting for the opportunity to take over the world.

Although I would personally have to accept this as one *possible* scenario for the future, the relentless hammering of the theme is hardly going to help young people to look objectively at contemporary history and current developments in East–West affairs, nor is it going to help them relate positively to any individual Russian citizen who might cross their paths.

One of the most disturbing side-effects of war toys is the fact that many can be used for real-life fighting.

> With their imaginations fuelled by kung fu cult films and violent movies like Rambo, youngsters are saving up pocket money to buy weapons like the ones used by their screen heroes. The police are appalled by the spread of the weapons, especially after the recent riots where the mob included armed 13-year-olds.[9]

A number of issues are raised by the debate, but several points emerge clearly.

1. There is a difference between imaginative play, using home-made resources, and play using sophisticated modern replicas

In personal terms, this would lead me as a parent to allow my children to play with wooden swords and Lego guns, but to ban highly-detailed replicas.

2. War toys seem to have a function in not only working out aggression, but also in neutralising it

A child fighting his friend and shouting 'Bang! You're dead!' may be becoming a less aggressive personality through doing so. As a parent, this reminds me that apparent conflict between two children need not necessarily be stopped.

3. Guns and war toys have an influence on children's minds

They convey attitudes and even political views. A parent should be constantly keeping an eye open for what is currently holding the interest of the child, and what the 'messages' are that the toy is conveying. A look through the toy cupboard might be a good idea, and a chat with the child about specific toys. It is often surprising what quite young children have deduced, from a toy, about the wider world.

What can we do about it?

On war toys, a good start is to contact the Peace Pledge Union.[10] The Children and War Project has the same address. They have a helpful leaflet of resources.

The debate about violent toys and war toys is just one area where Christians are faced with the values of the secular world and forced to make difficult choices (as are many who are not Christians, on this issue). Often the temptation for a Christian parent is to look for a Christian alternative to the whole secular toy world. Wouldn't it be better to turn one's back on the whole multi-billion dollar industry, and look for Christian toys, games and recreational facilities?

I have on my desk as I write two pieces of paper.

One is an advertisement for a new series of dolls from the creators of Care Bears.

> As a Mom, you want to raise your child with wholesome Christian values. Love. Friendship. Faith.
>
> And now, with Special Blessings dolls, you have a helping hand. These soft, huggable dolls have beautiful, silky hair and adorable outfits every child will love. But more than just playful friends, all four Special Blessings dolls capture the joy of prayer.
>
> So now your child can share her love, her friendship and her faith with a very special friend.[11]

The second is the current edition of the Case Reports of the Advertising Standards Authority, which records that:

> Two members of the public...objected to a national press mail order advertisement for a talking teddy bear which claimed "They can say anything...even your child's favourite bedtime prayer." The complainants, who purchased the bear, found that the speech facility was limited to a three-second period.[12]

What is interesting about these quite revolting toy advertisements is that they seem to be responding to the large Evangelical Christian market in America, which has tremendous buying power. The dream of many Christians is being realised; a number of Christian toy companies have been founded.

One of them, Rainfall, has produced a series of dolls called 'Bible Greats', which feature biblical heroes. The concept is an obvious imitation of series such as He-Man and the Masters of the Universe. The packaging, which offers a doll, a cassette tape and a book in a bubble pack, is very similar to the secular offering. The quality of the Rainfall dolls is not outstanding—all the men look very similar, as do the women. But all the dolls have clear biblical roles.

Rainfall have a series of collectable dolls called 'Kingdom Critters'.

> Kingdom Critters are cuddly-soft plush animals designed to demonstrate the attributes of familiar Bible characters! Each is delightfully dressed in an appropriate Bible-time costume and each represents a special trait:
>   Loyal Collie, who remains loyal like RUTH;
>   Adorable Angora, who shows inner beauty like ESTHER;
>   Eager Beaver, who is diligent like NOAH;
>   Courageous Lion, who stands courageous like DAVID.[13]

They have also produced a game, *Choices: a biblical approach to moral dilemmas*—again an obvious imitation of the secular game *Scruples*. The best-selling *Trivial Pursuit* has several Christian versions; Lawson Falle have published *Truth and Triumph*, acknowledging its ancestry by its advertising slogans: 'Tired of "trivial" pursuits? Try this stimulating new Bible knowledge game....' Other products available are a version of *Little Red Riding Hood* in which the heroine is converted and filled with the Holy Spirit.

The characteristic of this industry is that it seems to be attempting to replace every secular play resource with a Christianised equivalent. The implication is that there is absolutely nothing that the secular world of play can contribute to Christian childhood.

Such a position is one end of a scale, at the other end of which are those families that allow their children to play with anything at all, with possibly a few exceptions; and rely on the Christian values that they have taught their offspring to preserve them from danger.

In between the two extremes, which one might call fleeing the world and embracing the world, are many different approaches and perspectives.

Books about toys

The emerging Christian toy industry in America has produced a number of books which illustrate the underlying philosophy. I want to look briefly at three of them which are available in Britain.

Winkie Pratney's *Devil Take the Youngest*[14] is an excellent handbook on a wide range of disturbing abuses of children, packed with addresses and information. He devotes the first half of the book to an exposition of the occult roots of the war on childhood, which is hard going but places all that follows in a perspective of all-out demonic assault on children.

He is correct, I think, to see the current crisis of child abuse as part of a demonic attack on the world. However, I think in one or two places he tends to read more malign influence into some things than actually exists, and particularly when he talks about games and toys.

What Winkie Pratney's book illustrates about the American Christian view of toys is that it is based on a very strong commitment to the vulnerability of the child, and the preciousness of each individual in the eyes of God.

Fantasy Explosion, by Bob Maddux[15] covers a lot of ground, and says some discerning things about most of the subject he covers. Unfortunately he reveals in his first chapter a basic lack of sympathy and understanding for live fantasy role-playing (he clearly doesn't understand why people choose to do it), and this is apparent elsewhere in the book. He also seems to equate fantasy with sin, by identifying the serpent's lie in Eden as the first fantasy 'explosion'.

Nevertheless, his book indicates that the American toy industry is looking hard at a number of cultural areas, and he is helpful in basic biblical analysis. The main problem with the book is that much of his research is dated and uncritically handled.

Both books share a common perspective on toys: they argue that the toy industry is under a malign, satanic influence, and that that influence can be discerned in the products themselves.

Turmoil in the toybox

Such a perspective becomes, in the hands of Phil Phillips, an all-out attack on the entire Mattel/Hasbro empire.

Turmoil in the Toybox[16] is a frustrating book. It has more than a few helpful things to say, and in places—especially when discussing the place of TV in the home—Phillips is excellent. But the main thrust of the book is directed at the toy industry, and several of its conclusions are worrying. Also Phillips' approach is very intellectual, with comparatively little attention paid to how children actually play with the products he describes.

Phillips' case is that the toy industry is dominated by deliberate infiltration by occult and satanic agencies. He argues his case with a wealth of quotation from secular and Christian sources.

A good example is his discussion of My Little Pony.

> Because these toys are based on mythological creatures, they are occult. Mythology is in contradiction to God's Word. That is not the only problem with this series. Unicorns also are a symbol of the *New Age Movement*, which is in direct contradiction to Scripture.... The unicorn is a symbol of the anti-Christ, which the prophet Daniel described in his vision as the little horn which rises in the midst of the ten horns.[17]

He also draws attention to the presence of a rainbow in the toy's packaging, another 'symbol of New Age thinking'.

There is a great deal in the world of toys that needs biblical evaluation, but Phil Phillips raises a disturbing number of red herrings.

For example, mythology and the occult are not the same. Epimenides, who worshipped Zeus, was quoted with a measure of approval by Paul in Athens. Mythology is a failed attempt to reach God; the occult is a deliberate alternative to God.

Secondly, whatever New Agers make of it, the unicorn is traditionally a symbol for Christ, and his one horn was taken by medieval thinkers to represent the great doctrine that Christ was one with God. The rainbow, too, is perhaps second only to the cross as a Christian symbol.

Thirdly, the identification of the 'little horn' of Daniel 7 (referring to a beast with *eleven* horns) with the unicorn obscures the meaning of the passage (and a flying lion appeared in the same vision, which presumably means that C S Lewis's Aslan is an occult symbol...).

Readers will have gathered that I find many of the arguments in Phillips' book unconvincing. But it must be said that these arguments, particularly those of *Turmoil in the Toybox*, present us with a challenge and a problem.

The challenge is this: do we care about what our children play with? Do we recognise the fact that Satan can influence a child's mind through a toy just as much as he can an adult's through a book or a film? And do we care enough to want to change things—in our homes and in our toyshops?

It's a challenge that we would do well to listen to.

The problem is this: it is not enough simply to discard a whole secular toy industry as occult and replace it with a Christian version. By so doing we thereby lose the whole heritage of Western imaginative play, suffused though it be with weakened and trivialised Christian values and heavily over-commercialised. On the other hand, we bequeath to our children an inadequate basis for coming to terms with the world in which they will eventually have to live without us, where it will be necessary to make choices and distinctions.

My Little Pony and similar toys are neither ideal Christian play material nor explicit occult propaganda. The challenge they present to Christians is to decide what place they are to have in our families.

Some families will ban them; some, like my own, will give them a limited place and ensure that more biblical images are presented to the child as well. Some families will find a variety of Christian toys and dolls helpful; others will not. Many families will find the resources of an organisation like the British Toymakers Guild helpful in finding good quality alternatives to current plastic crazes.

The emphasis must surely be that the world of toys is not a neutral area. Toys reflect, to varying degrees, the world we live in—a world which is often opposed to the Christian gospel. And the toys, because they do communicate, sometimes communicate a little of that opposition.

10

Answering Back—How to Make Your Voice Heard

This last chapter is a resource chapter. It gives names and addresses of a number of organisations that are active in the toy industry. Whether you have a toy that has broken when it shouldn't have, a game that arrived with pieces missing, or a teddy bear whose eyes are mounted on lethal spikes, you will find here an address to begin making your discontent known.

But you will find here also information about organisations that exist to protect children against the subtler forms of danger we have been considering in this book, against those toys and games that actually adversely affect children's developing imaginations and cause problems. Such problems are not as explicitly dealt with in Acts of Parliament as questions of safety and consumer rights, but many parents are worried about them.

I've met many worried parents and teachers in different parts of the country. Whether in conversation with individuals, speaking to PTAs, teachers' or church groups, or simply reading the letters that arrive on my desk, I often hear the question, 'What can we *do* about some of the toys our children are playing with?' And it's a question I've also been asked in many places outside Britain.

Well, there is a lot we can do, and a number of places we can turn for help. But my first suggestion may be an unexpected one.

1. In the first instance, write positively!

Many of today's toys offer extensive play opportunities and much imaginative enrichment. Some of them are toys in categories that I haven't discussed in this book. Lego, for instance, has enabled several generations of children to construct satisfying fantasies for themselves, using plastic blocks and other pieces that on their own might seem very uninspiring. But the presentation, packaging and instructions show children how to use their imaginations—so that a few bricks inexpertly put together by a three-year-old can become a palace, a wheelbarrow, or a twenty-ton lorry.

My own children, and most of the many children I know, have had endless pleasure with Lego. Our own experience is that it's not too expensive, not least because the manufacturers have a very realistic attitude to providing replacements for lost pieces, and they also offer inexpensive packs of bulk parts. There are some very expensive Lego kits available, but one can go a long way towards them by buying individual parts out of pocket-money.

Then there's our climbing frame: it seemed horrendously expensive at the time (we tried not to think how many groceries we could have bought with the money), but our two children and dozens more have enjoyed it over the years, and it still stands in our garden, working—if not quite looking—as good as new.

Recently we invested in a similarly expensive toy, but one that seems to have the same potential for lasting pleasure: Playskool's Pipeworks, a life-size construction kit that lets children build their own trucks and ride in them, or eat their supper at a table they have made themselves. Well-made, thoughtfully designed, and supplied with very precise instructions to ensure maximum safety, this toy has already given lots of pleasure.

Every family has much-loved toys in the toy cupboard which have contributed to their children's growing imaginative fulfilment. In the case of our own toy cupboard, I can think of a jigsaw, a toy camera, a raggedy doll, the wonderfully creative modelling material Fimo, and many others.

In a very real sense, the designers and manufacturers of such toys are important in the lives of our children. Their products have made our children into more dextrous, more interested, more imaginative human beings. For the comparatively short time that their products are important to our children, they are our partners in parenting.

I'm grateful for the skills, vision, and commitment to children of a large number of people in the toy industry. I'm even grateful to them for advertising their products, which they do with all the expertise of modern advertising—these are manufacturing companies we're talking about, not registered charities—because otherwise we might not have come across them.

It must be said that even some of the products I've looked at critically in this book have given my children pleasure. I really do doubt whether My Little Pony magazine has ever either really interested or really helped them, but the toys themselves have demonstrated long-lasting play value and charm. Personally I find them appalling, but my children disagree! Money spent on them has given a good return in play. I don't think that, in recognising the limitations and even problems in that toy, one needs to be blinkered to the fact that they give children pleasure. If your children's experience of My Little Pony is the same, it would be quite reasonable to mention that fact if you were writing to Hasbro to register disquiet about other aspects of the toy.

Our family's own way of handling the Pony craze is strictly to limit the amount of money spent on the ponies, to resist passionate pleas to invest in the more expensive accessories, and to make good use of jumble sales to buy other children's cast-offs cheaply. But we have not banned them from the house, and we've tried to ensure that other more enriching toys were made available to them as well.

Customer feedback

So—if toys have given pleasure, and if some have played a major part in the developing of your child's imagination—write and tell the manufacturer!

From a business point of view, you're doing yourself and the company a favour. Toy manufacturers spend enormous amounts of money researching children's attitudes to their products, and customer reaction is usually taken seriously. Of course, as we have seen, several companies are multinational million-dollar enterprises, and hard-headed business dealing and the profit motive rule the boardroom as much as, if not more than, the play needs of children. But even in those companies, your letter will find its way on to somebody's desk and play a part in the company's evaluation of its product range. And if you are writing to express an objection to any part of the philosophy of the product, your comments will be taken much more seriously if they are balanced, acknowledging that your child didn't exactly have to be dragged, kicking and struggling, to play with the toy in the first place!

You may have a technical criticism of the toy—perhaps there is a task involved that is just too difficult for some small fingers, or the toy may have shed more paint than you think reasonable after only a few weeks' play. And your general impression of the toy is positive—you don't want to make an official complaint before you've written to the manufacturer about the problem (if matters reach a point where you *do* want to make a fuss, the addresses and information in the following pages should be useful).

Your criticism will be much more likely to be taken seriously if it is made in the light of your children's experience of regular and enthusiastic play. If it's a valid criticism, other users will probably have made it as well. Your contribution will add to the likelihood that the manufacturer will refer the matter to his designer for future reference, thus benefiting you and other parents in later purchases.

Job satisfaction

Writing a constructive letter in an appreciative and courteous manner is important in other ways. In my own contacts with the toy, game and comic industry over several years, I have found that a considerable number of people in that industry care deeply about children.

Although there are certainly plenty of cynical and money-orientated individuals, there are also people with a strong commitment to children—some of them have backgrounds in teaching, social work, or other educational and caring professions. Such people take real pleasure in knowing that their product is being enjoyed and appreciated.

They are also genuinely concerned if it is suggested that the product for which they are responsible might harm children, or indeed have anything but a positive influence. So if you have a valid criticism of the product, such people not only should be told—they *want* to be told.

2. State your case fully and calmly

How can you tell whether your letter will land on that sort of person's desk? You can't. That's why your letter should be calm, factual, backed up by examples (perhaps including the toy itself if, for example, it has broken in normal play) and positive in tone.

If the address of the manufacturer, designer or importer is not shown on the toy or its packaging, the reference section of your local public library will be able to trace it for you, given the name of the company.

If you have a complaint or criticism, address your letter to the Sales Department, or use the address provided if the instructions tell you how to return faulty goods. If you are writing simply to express appreciation, write to the 'Managing Director', unless you have been able to find the precise title for the chief executive of the company.

3. Make use of all the resources available

There will be occasions when a toy is defective, or dangerous, because of faulty workmanship or poor materials. If this is so, it may well be that a letter to the manufacturer will not be any use. The firm may be based abroad, or the standard of manufacture may prompt you to think about putting legal pressure on the makers rather than engaging in a dialogue. This would probably be the case if a toy was stuffed with a known flammable material, or a teddy's eyes were fixed loosely onto pointed spikes, or a set of face-paints produced painful skin irritation on any child who used them (and not just those with sensitive skin).

There are two issues here: first, your rights as a customer—you have spent money on these goods and are entitled to satisfaction; and second, public safety—other children will end up playing with them if the toys are permitted to continue on sale.

Your consumer rights

Your rights as purchaser are covered in the UK by the Sale of Goods Act, the Consumer Protection Act, a British Standard, and several Regulations and Officers such as Trading Standards Officers and Consumer Protection Officers.

There are three grounds for action under the Sale of Goods Act.

1. Goods must be of 'merchantable quality'—that is, fit for the purpose for which such goods are normally used. A toy boat with paint that came off when wet would clearly fail this test, as would a clockwork car with wheels that refused to revolve. (A number of other factors are taken into consideration as well: was the toy sold extremely cheaply, offered second-hand, or sold as faulty? If so, 'quality' is obviously a relative term!)

2. Goods must be as described on the box or in the retailer's posters, etc. If the box says that it contains an

Action Man with full space exploration equipment, all the equipment listed must be there.

3. If you tell the shop that you want to use the purchase for a specific purpose, and the toy is sold to you on that understanding, then *it must be suitable for that purpose.* If you are buying a video game on the assurance of the retailer that it will run on a Sony television, it must do so.[1]

If they fail on any of these grounds, you are entitled to return the goods. It is the retailer, not the manufacturer, who is obliged to give you satisfaction, and he or she should be informed as soon as the problem is apparent. If matters become complicated, you should consult your local Citizens' Advice Bureau, and, if necessary, your local Trading Standards Officer or Consumer Protection Officer, whose job is to enforce consumer legislation.[2] Your local Office will be listed in the telephone directory under your local Council. The Government Department that keeps a watch on trading matters is the Office of Fair Trading, whose address is:

Office of Fair Trading
Field House
15–25 Bream's Buildings
London EC4A 1PR.

Requests for information and literature should be addressed to Room 310c, Bream House; but check with your local Citizens' Advice Bureau first. They will be able to advise you whether a direct approach to the Office of Fair Trading is appropriate, or whether a more effective line of complaint is open to you. A leaflet[3] is available from your local Citizens' Advice Bureau which explains when it is appropriate for an individual to approach the Office of Fair Trading direct.

Public safety
Where problems with unsatisfactory toys mean that the toys in question are actually dangerous, and children are at risk from them, a number of people and organisations want to

know about it (not least, the Office of Fair Trading mentioned above, who have the power to place a total ban on the import and sale of specific toys).

The British toy industry has been a world pioneer in safety precautions. There are a range of legal requirements covering areas of potential trouble—for example poisonous paint, inflammable materials and sharp edges and points. But in addition, the Code of Safety Requirements for Children's Toys and Playthings (BS 3443), published in 1961 after collaboration between the British Standards Institution and the British Toy and Hobby Manufacturers' Association, was the first-ever toy safety standard.

Initially it was a voluntary Code, but it became the basis of Government legislation on toy manufacture. BS 3443 served as a model for other national standards. Today, BS 5665 takes its place, part of an international concern for child safety. A toy that conforms to this Standard will announce the fact on its label or packaging.

In 1987, the Consumer Safety Act gave the government the power to ban imported toys which are unsafe, and these powers have been used several times. The Consumer Protection Act of the same year obliged manufacturers to produce, and sell, only safe goods; so it is now illegal to sell an unsafe toy.

The 1987 legislation will be made much stronger in January 1990, when a new European Standard for toy safety comes into force. This will extend to all the Common Market countries, and will strengthen and increase the protection offered by the 1987 legislation.

Voluntary controls

Thus toys are the subject of wide-ranging Regulations, Standards, Acts of Parliament and EEC directives. Yet the media frequently report cases of children who have been harmed—in some tragic cases, killed—by dangerous toys.

The reason is that even with the best legal framework,

faulty toys can come into the country without anybody realising that they are dangerous until the first accident happens; British manufacturers, too, who have had a very good safety record in the past, can still make an error in design and produce a toy that is potentially dangerous or even lethal.

The British Toy and Hobby Manufacturers' Association

Recognising this, the major British toy manufacturers' association has launched its own initiative to improve safety standards.

> The British Toy and Hobby Manufacturers' Association (BTHA) which represents over 95 per cent of UK toy manufacturers is launching the 'Lion Mark' for toys made by its members. It's a requirement of BTHA membership that a manufacturer's toys must conform with the current British Standards, so all toys with the Lion Mark should conform.[4]

Which? magazine commented that buyers should remember that companies that were not members of the BTHA were not eligible to use the Lion Mark, but that their toys may well conform to BS 5665. So the presence of the mark guarantees that the Standard has been met, but its absence does not necessarily mean that a toy is unsafe.

The address of the British Toy and Hobby Manufacturers' Association is:

British Toy and Hobby Manufacturers' Association
80 Camberwell Road
London SE5 0EG.

The Association handles thousands of enquiries every year from its members, the press, the public, major suppliers and other trade associations. It is primarily concerned with advising members on new legislation, monitoring overseas business opportunities, organising overseas trade missions, negotiating and liaising, and other functions of a trade association.

But it also stages an annual trade toy fair, participates in

overseas fairs, publishes a specialist trade journal, and—
through its subsidiary the British Toy Council Ltd—
promotes safety standards in toys.[5] The BTHA would be a
particularly helpful source of advice on toys for the handicapped child, as this is a priority in the work of the Council
(though people who have a particular interest in toys and
games for disabled and handicapped children should certainly also contact ACTIVE, which is described at the end of
this chapter).

The British Toymakers Guild

Another organisation dedicated to maintaining standards in
the toy and games industries is the British Toymakers Guild.

The Guild was founded in 1955 with the aim of 'promotion
of good original design and craftsmanship in toymaking'. Its
membership includes craftsmen and craftswomen, toyshops,
designers, and others.

The Guild does not, in bestowing BTG approval on a toy,
officially endorse it as safe, for clearly explained reasons.

> The B.T.G. toy first and foremost is designed and made by
> craftsmen, of original design, regardless of whether it is meant
> for any particular age. Although we do have an interest in the
> safety of the toy, the maker and designer will be, at all times,
> legally responsible for its safety aspect.[6]

Nevertheless, for parents who are tired of buying mass-
produced plastic and television-orientated toys, the Guild's
catalogue is an exciting resource. Membership is open to
individuals, and two toy fairs are held annually; a Trade Fair
in January, and a Christmas Fair in November. The latter is
open to the public.

Catalogues can be purchased, and membership and details
of the toy fairs obtained, from:

The Chairman
British Toymakers Guild
33 Hertford Avenue
East Sheen
London SW14 8EF.

Other organisations

Other trade organisations are the Toy and Giftware Importers Association (TGIA). Fifty-seven companies involved in importing are members. Its address is:

Toy and Giftware Importers Association
4th Floor
Artillery House
Artillery Row
London SW1P 1RT.

But enquiries and complaints from the public relating to imported toys are probably best dealt with by the statutory and legal bodies mentioned earlier. And the National Association of Toy Retailers (33 Sevenoaks Road, Orpington, Kent) is a trade association for the retail toy and allied trades.

Invisible risks

It will be clear from the foregoing that there is a great deal of help available for people who have made unsatisfactory purchases or who have reason to suspect that a toy is unsafe. In fact, in such matters Britain has an excellent record.

But what help is available for those who consider that a toy or game will cause problems for children at a deeper level than that of physical damage?

4. Be aware of published Codes of Practice

Advertising, as we have seen in an earlier chapter, is a particularly strong influence on the young, and also one where parents can easily recognise the vulnerability of their children. The vast amount of money invested in trying to attract and sway the youth market, and the commercial prizes at stake, mean that this is an area where control is essential.

The IBA Code of Practice

Advertising on television is controlled by the Independent Broadcasting Authority's Code of Advertising Standards and Practice, Appendix 1 of which covers 'Advertising and Children'. Paragraph 1 sets out its general thrust:

> No product or service may be advertised, and no method of advertising may be used, in association with a programme intended for children or which large numbers of children are likely to see or hear, which might result in harm to them physically, mentally or morally, and no method of advertising may be employed which takes advantage of the natural credulity and sense of loyalty of children. Children's ability to distinguish between fact and fantasy will vary according to their age and individual personality. With this in mind, no unreasonable expectation of performance of toys and games must be simulated by the excessive use of imaginary backgrounds or special effects.[7]

There is a wide range of detailed requirements in the Code. For example, television advertisements must not imply that a child is inferior, or lacks a sense of duty, or is disloyal, if he or she does not possess the product being advertised. They must not show children doing anything that would be dangerous if imitated in real life. And they must not 'directly urge children to purchase or to ask their parents or others to make enquiries or purchases'.

The Oracle teletext service which can be received by many television sets is also controlled by an IBA Code,[8] and Section B, on advertisements, has a clause relating to children. This forbids advertising of certain products on editorial pages in which children are likely to have a particular interest.

The existence of the IBA Code means that every advertisement that appears on British television has been scrutinised and judged acceptable. However, like most media guidelines, the Code is sometimes more effective in theory than in practice, and occasionally advertisements appear on television that are unacceptable.

When this happens, complain! We have seen already in Chapter 7 the case of the Tonka Supernaturals advertising campaign in 1987, when a large number of viewers objected and the advertisements were stopped. So if you have a complaint about an advertisement on television or commercial radio, write to:

The Advertising Division
Independent Broadcasting Authority
70 Brompton Road
London SW3 1EY.

Complaints about advertisements on cable or satellite television should be made to:

The Cable Authority
Gillingham House
38–44 Gillingham Street
London SW1 1HU.

If you have complaints about programme content (as opposed to individual advertisements between programmes), the same addresses can be used. If you need to complain to the BBC about programme content, write to:

BBC Television
Television Centre
Lime Grove
Shepherd's Bush
London W12 7RG.

Address your letter to the producer of the programme, whose name can be found in the *Radio Times*. Complaints about programme content on ITV should be made to the producer at your regional ITV company, whose address can be obtained from your local library. Channel 4's address is:

Channel 4 Television Company
60 Charlotte Street
London W1P 2AX.

Don't forget to praise as well as blame. The published Codes and Guidelines show considerable awareness of the vulnerability of children, and in a large number of instances television has served the needs and welfare of children well.

The Advertising Standards Authority

Advertisements in general are covered by the *British Code of Advertising Practice*.

> Advertisements should contain nothing which might result in physical, mental or moral harm to children, or which exploits their credulity, lack of experience, or sense of loyalty.[9]

The specific requirements cover the same areas as the other Codes mentioned earlier—for example, no advertisement should suggest that children not buying the product are failing in their duty, or exaggerate what an ordinary child can achieve with the product being advertised. There is also a strong emphasis on safety (for example, children should not be encouraged to talk to strangers in an attempt to collect coupons, wrappers etc).

The Advertising Standards Authority was set up by the advertising industry as a self-regulatory body. It deals with advertisements in the press, posters, cinema and on video. It publishes Case Reports which document complaints received about specific advertisements and action taken—usually, if the complaint is upheld, the advertiser is requested to amend or remove the advertisements; if he refuses to do so, the ASA reports the matter in full to the media.

If you find an advertisement that you feel is unacceptable, write to the Authority at:

Advertising Standards Authority Ltd.
Brook House
2–16 Torrington Place
London WC1E 7HN.

Give as many details as you can, and, if possible, enclose the advertisement. Remember, too, that some complaints fall more within the scope of other bodies.

> There are many legal provisions which affect the form and the content of advertisements.
>
> If you think that an advertisement breaks the Trade Descriptions Acts, the Race Relations Act or the Sexual Discrimination Act, for example, you should pass your complaint on to the proper authorities.[10]

5. Be prepared to campaign if necessary

Sometimes, when you have approached the proper authorities, lobbied professional organisations and talked to local retailers, a problem has still not been resolved. In such cases it is often helpful to turn to organisations of a more campaigning nature.

Two Christian organisations that have been very active campaigners are the Evangelical Alliance and CARE Campaigns.

The Evangelical Alliance

The Evangelical Alliance is an alliance of churches, denominations, parachurch societies and individuals. It therefore represents a very large Christian constituency, and has successfully acted on a number of child-related issues (for example, it was instrumental in persuading the London Dungeon museum to alter some of its very frightening tableaux which were being seen by a large number of children, some on school outings).

It has published leaflets on a number of issues, has

engaged in discussion with the media on subjects including Hallowe'en and children's fantasy literature, and provides a magazine and other services to its membership.

The EA in conjunction with other organisations has been responsible for some very influential conferences and seminars, including one on Reaching Tomorrow's Children. Most of the Christian organisations dealing with young people in Britain are part of the Evangelical Alliance.

The address of the Alliance is:

Evangelical Alliance
Whitefield House
186 Kennington Park Road
London SE11 4BT.

CARE

Christian Action Research and Education (CARE) supports Christian standards in society and co-ordinates practical caring initiatives throughout Britain. CARE Trust and CARE Campaigns work at grassroots and parliamentary level, are strong in research and co-ordinate the work of local core groups, church representatives, and other individuals supporting the work and projects of CARE.

CARE is active in a number of areas of concern for children. It is, for example, committed to strengthening the quality of Britain's educational system, specifically in the areas of religious and moral education, school assemblies and school governors.

Through its Child Protection Campaign, activities which indirectly benefit children (such as 'Picking up the Pieces', an anti-pornography campaign), and the recently launched CARE for the Family (a campaign to strengthen family life, in harmony with James Dobson's USA organisation Focus on the Family), CARE is involved in fighting a number of abuses against children. Several of their projects touch on matters we have looked at in this book.

CARE's address is:

CARE
53 Romney Street
London SW1P 3RF

Familybase

Children, of course, do not exist as independent social units—they are part of families. The family is under pressure from many directions today, and organisations which exist to strengthen and support family life are thereby helping children.

A Christian organisation doing this is Familybase, which exists for the strengthening of family life in Britain. It has pursued a number of concerns; particularly criticising the recent Sunday trading legislation proposals, and making proposals for legislative action on family debt. A part of Familybase is the registered charity Familybase Trust, which is concerned with education and family networks.

Information about Familybase and its activities can be obtained from:

Jubilee House
3 Hooper Street
Cambridge CB1 2NZ.

National Family Trust

An organisation not specifically Christian, but with aims with which Christians will identify, is the non-sectarian, non-political charity National Family Trust, which sponsors the National Campaign for the Family. Basing its view of the family on the centrality of marriage, it seeks to be 'a respected voice for families' among the public and among policy-makers, and to 'publicise topical and research-informed practical policies to meet the needs of families'.[11]

It has a list of policy objectives in a number of areas of

family life, and has published a book, *Families Matter*. Information can be obtained from:

The National Family Trust
c/o The Salvation Army (Legal Section)
101 Queen Victoria Street
London EC4P 4EP.

The Conservative Family Campaign

Although this organisation is obviously identified with a political party, it has produced material which has been helpful to many people working in the field of family pastoral work. With a strong focus on Westminster, as you would expect, they have published a range of material which has often made available information that would otherwise be difficult to get hold of. I think it is fair to say that their material is recognisably on the right wing of the political spectrum, but they are by no means a rubber-stamp organisation for the Government.

They can be contacted at the following address:

The Chairman
Conservative Family Campaign
45 West Hill Avenue
Epsom
Surrey KT19 8JX.

There are a number of other organisations active in matters that concern the physical and spiritual welfare of children. There is a useful list in *Children Under Pressure*, by Pat Wynnejones.[12]

Such organisations may be invaluable if their work has explored a subject which is of great concern to you as a parent. But you may want to consider supporting their work even if you do not need their help specifically at the moment. The history of children's welfare is full of organisations like them, which have pioneered often unpopular causes and secured the rights of children for future generations. Most of the organisations mentioned above have local groups or local representatives, and if you care about children, you may well want to get involved yourself.

6. Shout as loud as necessary

If you are still having difficulty in gaining satisfaction, you should consider your local MP or Euro-MP, and also contacting one of the media watchdog consumer programmes, such as Esther Rantzen's *That's Life!* (BBC1), Radio 4's *You and Yours*, or one of the investigative programmes such as those of Roger Cook.

Often television audience-participation programmes give an opportunity for the public to speak on issues of children's play—*Kilroy* (BBC) often debates child-related issues, and *The Time... The Place* (ITV) has had a discussion on toys. Where you think that something on television has been unhelpful to children, or may have harmed them, audience feedback programmes such as *Open Air* (BBC1) or *Right to Reply* (Channel 4) give you, the viewer, the opportunity to complain direct to the people who made the programme.

The National Toy Libraries Association/Play Matters

Having looked at a number of organisations which have a role to play in protecting the child from harm, I want to look at one which has as its primary purpose the extending of children's play opportunities and making toys accessible to children who otherwise would not have many available.

The first toy library in Britain was opened in 1967, by a mother who was a trained teacher and wanted to provide a variety of toys for children with different disabilities. From small beginnings, with parents exchanging toys from their own families, the idea snowballed, attracting media interest and numerous enquiries. In 1972, The Toy Libraries Association was founded, which is today the National Toy Libraries Association. It draws on a wide range of expertise in all aspects of child development, and fills an important role:

> Toy libraries exist to promote the principle that play *does matter* to the developing child. They operate as a preventative service, filling gaps in the existing provision for all families with babies and young children and for people with special needs. By offering a befriending, supportive service to parents and by making available and lending appropriate toys, they extend the opportunity for shared play into the home.[13]

Toy libraries are to be found in nursery and infants' schools, book libraries, hospitals, community centres and many other places. Often they are staffed by volunteers and run by parents. Mobile toy libraries exist serving some out-of-the-way places, and also for housebound children.

The Association publishes a magazine, *Ark*, and organises various events and links with other organisations. It also works closely with its associate organisation, ACTIVE.

ACTIVE

ACTIVE was founded in 1975 to explore ways of producing new toys and equipment for disabled children, and of modifying existing toys. Today there are many ACTIVE groups, extending the horizons of play and leisure activity for children and adults. The groups include teachers, therapists and toy designers, and there is also considerable interest in the application of computers to children with special needs.

ACTIVE groups often co-operate with local schools, and usually develop close links with the local toy library. Among their activities is the publication of worksheets showing how to make or adapt play and equipment.

In 1983 ACTIVE merged with the Toy Libraries Association, and the overall name Play Matters was chosen. Details of Play Matters, and their very useful publications mail order list, can be obtained from:

Play Matters
68 Churchway
London NW1 1LT.

7. Pray a great deal

We live in a time when many people and organisations are
fighting for the rights of children. But we also live in a time
when the lucrative children's market has attracted pressure
upon children that is unlike anything we have previously seen.

Some of the pressures are part and parcel of living in a
fallen world, and our task as parents is to help them to come
to terms with pressure and learn how to overcome it. Other
pressures are the result of vested business interests, or of the
activities of people who from a range of motives end up
producing resources which harm children. Our responsibility
then is to pursue any avenue we can to try to force the people
concerned to stop.

In either case, Christian parents—and I write as a Christian parent with Christian parents in mind here—will draw
their strength from the fact that this is not simply a struggle
between the individual and the corporation, the lone voice
against the mass-produced product. It is an aspect of the
cosmic struggle in which we are all involved, and in which all
mankind fights on one side or the other.

We do not go unarmed into that struggle. We are not
forced to defend our children with mere human strength.
That is why prayer, for the Christian parent, will always be
the strongest weapon in our armoury. For that is how we call
on the Lord our God, whose promise of the future includes a
vision of children at play.

> This is what the Lord Almighty says: "Once again men and
> women of ripe old age will sit in the streets of Jerusalem, each
> with cane in hand because of his age. The city street will be filled
> with boys and girls playing there" (Zechariah 8:4–5, NIV).

Notes

Introduction

1 *Haunted Wood* (Ravensburger, distr. in the UK by Fisher-Price, 1983).
2 David Porter, *Children at Risk* (Kingsway, 1986: 2nd edn 1987).

A Note on Language

1 In Dorothy Einon, *Creative Play* (Viking, 1985).

Chapter 1: Some Early Play Experiences

1 David and Tricia Porter, *Through the Eyes of a Child* (Lion, 1983), p. 1.
2 The term 'development' has a precise meaning in child psychology, where the distinction between development and growth is an important one. I am writing as a non-specialist, and shall be using the word in its everyday meaning to describe the process by which an infant gradually becomes an adult person in every aspect of its being.
3 Peter Coveney, *The Image of Childhood* (Peregrine, 1967), pp. 40–41.
4 The importance of adult–baby interaction as part of the learning process is emphasised by most writers on childhood. A very readable discussion is in John Holt, *How Children Learn* (Penguin, 1970). The subject is handled in different ways by people holding different views on the nature of personality and by people using the

179

child as data for an investigation into human personality, e.g. Muriel Beadle, *A Child's Mind: How Children Learn During the Critical Years from Birth to Age Five Years* (Methuen, 1971). The significance of the interaction seems however to be generally agreed.

5 See e.g. Dorothy Einon, *Creative Play* (Viking, 1985), 'From birth to two years', pp. 14 ff.

6 *Ibid*.

7 Catherine Garvey, *Play: the Developing Child* (Fontana/Open Books, 1977), p. 30.

8 D. W. Winnicott, *Playing and Reality* (Penguin, 1971), p. 119. This quotation is part of a discussion of 'potential space' between the child and its environment, in which, Winnicott argues, a child's play-learning takes place.

9 E. M. Matterson, *Play With a Purpose for Under-Sevens* (Penguin, 1965).

10 The growing child's relationship with television images is covered in a number of studies, e.g. Patricia Marks Greenfield, *Mind and Media: The Effects of Television, Computers and Video Games* (Fontana, 1984).

11 D. W. Winnicott, 'Roots of Aggression', *The Child, the Family and the Outside World* (1964), in: Clare Winnicott, Ray Shepherd and Madeleine Davis (eds), *D. W. Winnicott: Deprivation and Delinquency* (Tavistock Publications, 1984), p. 96.

12 Bruno Bettelheim, *A Good Enough Parent* (Penguin, 1987), p. 227.

13 Johan Huizinga, *Homo Ludens: a Study of the Play Element in Culture* (1949: repr. Paladin, 1970), p. 30.

Chapter 2: Heroes and Role Models

1 Enid Blyton, *Third Year at Malory Towers* (1948: repr. Granada, 1967), p. 25.

2 Pat Wynnejones, *Children under Pressure: Growing Up in a Changing World* (SPCK Triangle, 1987), pp. 77–78.

3 Enid Blyton, *The Twins at St Clare's* (1941: repr. Granada, 1967), p. 57.

4 C. S. Lewis, 'The Inner Ring', in *Transposition and Other Addresses* (Geoffrey Bles, 1949), p. 58. He also has some good

things to say about collective identity in the context of church life in 'Membership', in *Fernseed and Elephants* (Fontana, 1975), pp. 11–25.

5 *Number One*, 16 April 1988, pp. 10–11.

6 *My-Guy*, 2 August 1986, p. 9.

7 Chapter 2 of my *Children at Risk* (Kingsway, rev. edn 1987) deals with some of these problems.

8 *Blue Jeans*, 2 August 1986, front cover.

9 Much of this material is published in my book *User's Guide to The Media* (IVP, 1988).

10 Philippians 3:12–14,17, NIV.

Chapter 3: A World without Morals?

1 Aldous Huxley, 'The Giaconda Smile' in *Mortal Coils*, (1922: repr. Chatto & Windus, 1925), p. 46.

2 *My Little Pony* comic, 23 February 1989, advertisement.

3 Kenneth Grahame, 'A Departure', in: *Dream Days* (1898: Nelson edn, n.d), pp. 270–271.

4 Michael Buhler, *Tin Toys 1945–1975* (Bergstrom and Boyle, 1978), p. 1.

5 J. H. P. Pafford, ed., *Isaac Watts: Divine Songs* (Oxford University Press, 1971), 'Introduction 3: the Man and his Work...', p. 23.

6 'Patrick Rylands' Penny Toys', interview in the catalogue of the 3rd London International Antique Toy and Doll Convention, 1982.

7 For example the issue of 3 December 1988 has a lead story about the toys putting on a concert, a cut-out background for the child to make and pose the toys against, and a practical project for making music out of household objects. Also the quality of the artwork in this comic is superior to the others mentioned in this chapter.

8 My Little Pony Club advertisement, 1989.

9 *Barbie Magazine*, August 1986, p. 31.

10 Chris Walker, 'Hype Versus Traditionalism', in *What Toy?* 1977–88, p. 102.

11 Phil Phillips, *Turmoil in the Toybox* (Starburst, 1986: distr. in UK by Diasozo Trust).

Chapter 4: The World of Right and Wrong

1 George Perry and Alan Aldridge, *The Penguin Book of Comics* (Penguin, 1967 rev. edn 1971), p. 171.

2 *The Origin of He-Man*, given free with *Masters of the Universe Adventure Magazine*, No. 12, 1989.

3 Les Keyser, *Hollywood in the Seventies*, quoted in: Leslie Halliwell, *Halliwell's Film Guide* (5th edn, Paladin 1977), p. 922.

4 I have given a description of such games, and an analysis of the debate that surrounds them, in *Children at Risk* (2nd edn, Kingsway, 1987), p. 85 ff.

5 Computerdial Ltd advertisement, January 1989.

6 'G.M. Interview: Gygax', *G.M.*, January 1989, p. 14.

7 *Children at Risk*, pp. 99 ff.

8 'Judge's Manual', p. 21, from *Judge Dredd: the Role-Playing Game* (Games Workshop UK, 1985).

Chapter 5: Half-way Heroes

1 Avalon Hill 1984 advertisement for the launch of their fantasy role-playing magazine *Heroes*.

2 Martin Barker, *A Haunt of Fears: the Strange History of the British Horror Comics Campaign* (Pluto Press, 1984).

3 I would say, for example, that *Bad Timing* featured sexual brutality and a highly brutal, visible and erotic murder; that *Tom and Jerry*'s violence is always followed by evidence that nobody was really hurt; that *The A-Team* operates in the Wild-West type of mythology where 'everyone gets shot and nobody gets hurt'; and that most viewers of *Rocky* recognise that the bloodstained finale is at least taking place in a boxing ring and that physical pain is what success in sport requires. (All of which leaves unanswered some important questions about suitability for, and access by, children.)

4 Confirmed in a conversation between Mr Bright and myself in 1985.

5 *Care Bears*, 28 January 1989, p. 3.

6 *The Care Bears Family: 'The Long Lost Care Bears' and 'Bravest of the Brave'*, video recording copyrighted 1986 by Those Characters From Cleveland Inc., released in the UK by Virgin Video.

7 Examples taken from *Care Bears* (issue noted in no. 5 above, p.

11) and 'Bravest of the Brave' (second feature on the video noted in no. 6 above).

8 John Grant, *Masters of the Universe: Castle Grayskull Under Attack!* (Ladybird Books, 1984), p. 10.

9 John Grant, *She-ra Princess of Power: She-ra and the Dark Pool* (Ladybird Books, 1985), p. 19.

10 Quoted in Roger Kean, 'Daily Planet: the Never-Ending Story', *LM*, January 1987, p. 29.

11 'And graves give up their dead...', *Superman*, No. 19, 1989, p. 9.

12 Advertisement in *Transformers*, 16 May 1987, p. 16. The toy has since reverted to its original name *Optimus Prime*.

13 'Judge's Manual', p. 2, from *Judge Dredd: the Role-Playing Game* (Games Workshop UK, 1985).

Chapter 6: Playing with Problems

1 Sue Townsend, *The Adrian Mole Diary 1986* (Two-Can Design, 1985), entries for 17 Jan., 12 July.

2 Interview with Evelyne Kestemberg, in: Anne Clancier and Jeannine Kalmanovitch, *Winnicott and Paradox: from Birth to Creation* (Tavistock Publications, 1987), p. 131.

3 Quoted, by permission, from an unpublished paper by Malcolm Doney.

4 James Dobson, *Discipline While You Can: the Strong-Willed Child* (Kingsway, 1978), p. 182.

5 Benjamin Spock, *Baby and Child Care* (New English Library edition, 1975), p. 376.

6 James Dobson, *Discipline While You Can*, p. 183.

7 I received a letter from a major fantasy game manufacturer after the publication of *Children at Risk*, expressing agreement with much of the book and appreciation of the fact that fantasy games had been discussed as part of a range of influences. Much valid criticism is discounted because it is focused on one aspect of a problem.

8 Roger Hurding, *Understanding Adolescence* (Hodder, 1989), pp. 10–11.

9 *Blue Jeans & Patches*, 25 February–4 March 1989, p. 2.

10 Readership ages quoted in this chapter were obtained by telephoning the advertising managers of the publications concerned.

11 *Eagle and Mask*, 4 March 1989, centre pages and back cover.

12 Muriel Beadle, *A Child's Mind: How Children Learn During the Critical Years from Birth to Age Five Years* (Methuen, 1972), pp. 171, 196, 216.

13 Jack Tinker, 'What does Madonna really wannabee?', *Daily Mail*, 17 August 1987. Tinker is the *Mail*'s theatre critic.

14 'Zapchat', by John Riglar, in *Sinclair User*, January 1989, p. 16.

15 'Zapchat', *Sinclair User*, November 1988, p. 18.

16 In the June 1989 issue, published as this book was being proofread, it was announced that Ms Maughan was handing over the editorship to Matt Goss.

17 'Kindly leave the stage', *Your Sinclair*, January 1988, p. 15.

18 *Your Sinclair*, May 1988.

19 'Letters', *Your Sinclair*, May 1988, p. 14.

20 'Advice', *Just Seventeen*, 13 April 1988, p. 22.

21 A helpful survey of teenage magazines, with good analysis of their advice columns, is Joanna Bogle (ed), *The Seductive Sell: A Look at Today's Teenage Magazines* (The Responsible Society Research and Education Trust, 1986). The Society's address is Wicken, Milton Keynes MK19 6BU.

Chapter 7: The First Kid on the Block

1 *Masters of the Universe* comic, No. 10, 1986, inside front cover.

2 *My Little Pony* comic, No. 91, 1986, inside back cover.

3 I have discussed the techniques and messages of advertising in *User's Guide to the Media* (IVP, 1988), pp. 36–49.

4 'Teddies' festive challenge to robots', *Daily Express*, 10 December 1987.

5 Mattel UK, *Masters of the Universe* poster/advertisement for MOTU dolls, c. 1986.

6 The information on Kenner products is taken from a report reproduced in McCarthy Information Ltd's card of 4 December 1987.

7 Daily Telegraph 8 October 1988.

8 'Socialisation' in *The Young, New Society*'s social science brief, 14 February 1986. In Chapter 1 of *Children at Risk* I discuss young

people as a market, though the recent changes in British employment figures and the economy in general have altered the picture somewhat.

9 *Marketing*, 1 October 1987.

10 Quoted in Vance Packard, *The Hidden Persuaders* (Penguin, 1957), p. 135.

11 *Ibid.*, p. 17.

12 Figures taken from 'How Hasbro Became King of the Toy-makers', *Business Week*, 22 September 1986.

13 Figures taken from *Marketing*, 9 June 1988.

14 Figures taken from 'How Hasbro Became King of the Toy-makers', see n. 12.

15 See Brian Rotman, 'Toying with the Audience', *The Listener*, 9 October 1986.

16 Peggy Charren, paper delivered at 'Television and the Family: a new Agenda', Conference organised by the British Film Institute and the University of London Institute of Education, February 1987.

17 I am indebted to a correspondent for this quotation from a British daily newspaper. I have not been able to trace details of its source.

18 *Marketing Week*, 20 November 1987.

19 'Playing for Airtime', *Which?*, December 1988, p. 561.

20 'Toys to Play with Television', *New Scientist*, 12 March 1987.

21 See note 16.

22 *Marketing*, 11 February 1988.

23 *Marketing Week*, 10 June 1988.

24 'The TV Programme That Shoots Back', *Daily Mail*, 18 September 1987.

25 *Financial Post*, 20 October 1988.

26 Peter Brown, 'Hype Versus Traditionalism', in *What Toy?*, 1987–88, p. 100.

27 Ian McMurtrie, 'A Manufacturer's View', *What Toy?*, 1978–88, p. 101.

Chapter 8: The Seduction of the Innocent

1 Jane Bird and Rosemary Collins, 'Children Tune into Computer Porn by Phone', *Sunday Times*, 12 March 1989.

2 From Tony Horgan's review in *Amiga User International*, March 1989, p. 20.

3 The programmer is identified on the bulletin board as Jan Wesener of Rudeware Productions in the USA.

4 Jane Bird and Rosemary Collins, *op. cit.*

5 'Age Is No Bar for On-line Porn', *Datalink*, 27 February 1989, p. 3.

6 'Stop This Disgrace: Sick and Racist Game', *New Computer Express*, 11 March 1989, p. 3.

7 'Pirates Peddle Race Hatred', *Datalink*, 6 March 1989, p. 3.

8 Glyn Ford, 'Foul Play in the Games Market', *Computing*, 5 January 1989.

9 From the cover of a 1985 *Scream!* special. I discussed this issue at length in *Children at Risk*, pp. 123 ff.

10 *Viz*, August/September 1988.

11 This has been argued persuasively by Mike Alsford, a Christian critic: in 'The British Comic Comeback', *Strait Magazine*, Spring 1989, p. 32.

12 Cf. Martin Barker (ed.), *The Video Nasties: Freedom and Censorship in the Media* (Pluto Press, 1984).

13 Bob Maddux, *Fantasy Explosion* (Regal Books, 1986), p. 45.

Chapter 9: War Toys, and Christian Options

1 Article by Jill Tweedie, *The Guardian*, 30 November 1981.

2 I believe that this excellent game published by Avalon Hill USA is no longer available.

3 Richard Hamblen responding to Martin Williams, 'Letters to the Editor', *The General*, Vol. 20 No. 5, 1984, p. 45.

4 Dorothy Einon, *Creative Play* (Viking, 1985), p. 106.

5 Bruno Bettelheim, *A Good Enough Parent* (Pan, 1988), p. 279.

6 Peace Pledge Union, leaflet *Playing with War* (PPU, 1987).

7 I am indebted to Zygote's monthly column in *Computer Express*, November 1988, p. 152, for the information in this paragraph.

8 Richard Seel, *'Video Game Nasties?'*, *ST World*, p. 80.

9 'Killers over the Counter', *Mail on Sunday*, 27 October 1985.

10 The Peace Pledge Union, 6 Endsleigh Street, London WC1.

11 1988 advertisement (USA) for Special Blessing dolls from Those Characters From Cleveland Inc.

12 Advertising Standards Authority, *Case Report 167*, 15 March 1989, p. 11.

13 From Rainfall's catalogue.

14 Winkie Pratney, *Devil Take the Youngest: the War on Childhood* (Huntington House, 1985), distributed in the UK by Diasozo Trust.

15 Bob Maddux, *Fantasy Explosion* (Regal Books, 1986), distributed in the UK by Regal's London office.

16 Phil Phillips, *Turmoil in the Toybox* (Starburst, 1986), distributed in the UK by Diasozo Trust.

17 *Ibid.*, p. 79.

Chapter 10: Answering Back—How to Make Your Voice Heard

1 The description of the provisions of the Act is based on *How to Put Things Right*, a booklet published for the Office of Fair Trading and the Central Office of Information (HMSO, July 1988), p. 5.

2 The Fair Trading structure is explained in *Office of Fair Trading: How It Works*, a leaflet prepared by the Office of Fair Trading and the Central Office of Information (HMSO, November 1988).

3 See note 2.

4 *Which?*, December 1988, p. 572.

5 Information on BTHA is taken from its *Membership Information Pack*.

6 From the Constitution of the British Toymakers Guild.

7 'Advertising and Children', Appendix 1 of *The IBA Code of Advertising Standards and Practice* (IBA, July 1986 repr.), p. 7.

8 *The IBA Code for Teletext Transmissions* (IBA, 1984).

9 *The British Code of Advertising Practice*, Sec. B.20, p. 33. The Code was first published in 1961.

10 *It's Easy to Complain About Advertisements. But Which Ones?* Undated leaflet from the ASA.

11 *Families in Danger* (National Family Campaign, undated booklet), p. 4.

12 Pat Wynnejones, *Children Under Pressure: Growing Up in a Changing World* (SPCK Triangle, 1987), pp. 175–178.

13 From the *Play Matters* leaflet, issue current in March 1989.

Children at Risk

by David Porter

Our children—precious, inquisitive, vulnerable

This is an exciting age for children, where whole worlds of fantasy games, books and computers can be explored. Cinema and television excel in spectacular entertainment and stimulating education.

But there are risks.

David Porter, author and parent, takes us through some of the products and influences that are winning the minds of our children. While welcoming the wealth of creativity that so many bring, he sounds important warning notes for all those who wish to protect children from the nastier and more sinister elements of the market place. Finally we are alerted to the increasing physical danger our children face, as David looks at the unspoken risk of sexual abuse and the sale of drugs to under-fifteen-year-olds.

Parents and teachers will find this book a mine of information as well as a stirring manifesto for action. Brilliantly researched yet easy to read, it steers a course between the twin extremes of ill-advised panic and foolish complacency, showing us where the dangers lie and where we can tread the ground more confidently.

 Kingsway Publications